TALES
FROM
- THE -
CANCER
WARD

Dear Agnes —
As promised — it is such
a truly loving of life book,
with so many deep & well written
thoughts. I hope you enjoy it
as much as I have.
My deep love,
Felys   12/11.
(Co-Mum!)

Also by Paul Cox

Home of the Man: the people of New Guinea with Uli Beier Nelson 1971

Human Still Lives from Nepal S.I. 1971

Mirka with Uli Beier Macmillan 1980

Vincent: the life and death of Vincent van Gogh. Study notes for the film.
Australian Teachers of Media 1987

I Am with Wim Cox 1997

Three Screenplays: Lonely Hearts, My First Wife, A Woman's Tale.
Currency 1998

Reflections: an autobiographical journey Currency 1998

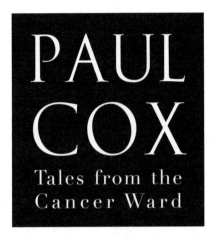

PAUL COX

Tales from the Cancer Ward

With a Foreword by Roger Ebert
and an Introduction by John Larkin

transit lounge

First Published 2011
Transit Lounge Publishing
95 Stephen Street
Yarraville, Australia 3013
www.transitlounge.com.au
info@ transitlounge.com.au

Cover image: Paul Cox
Author photograph: Kyra Cox

Design by Peter Lo

Printed in China by Everbest
ISBN 978-0-9808462-3-2

Cataloguing in Publication entry is available from the
National Library of Australia: http://catalogue.nla.gov.au

For all those who quietly
go about saving lives

Paul, when they had cut me up and harvested my body to patch up the damage, you called my wife Chaz to say you had dreamed about me. In the hospital the next day she gave me this news and I remember her crying, although your dream contained good omens. She cried because she loved you and you cared, and at a certain point in illness care is the only thing we have. Care for those we love, care for ourselves. Of all the people I have met in this life, you seem to care the most. Your fierce anger leaps out at injustice, bigotry and stupidity. You rightly condemn in these pages the way we live now. You write: 'Some people spend a lifetime in a job they don't like, living a life they don't want, and the money they earn is spent on things they don't need.' You have not done that. You have made it your business not to. You care that others not waste their lives.

Reading these pages, I found you mentioning experiences I must have had and cannot remember. My troubles were often a blur, and weeks have disappeared into a fog of medication and confusion. When they were taking me home from hospital after my first surgery, a carotid artery ruptured. 'They thought we had lost you,' Chaz told me. 'They thought you were dead.' She refused to believe it. She told them I was still alive, and I was communicating with her. I am writing these words, so she must have been right. She called you to discuss these things, and emails passed back and forth while for me the only reality was the hospital routine you describe: the tests, the gowns, the nakedness before strangers, the cries from another bed, the endless checks of the 'vitals'. Yes, my heart was beating. Yes, the plastic clamp on my finger found oxygen in my blood.

You write about that so well. You spent your years in good health and curiosity, discovering in Australia you had the spirit of a dreamer and a traveller. You loved and were loved. You had three children you are proud of. Although in my imagination they might have been raised in a household like that in *My First Wife*, it must have been a house with intelligence and passion in it. And you were the workman, upstairs over the store, still using his old tools. 'The good workman respects his tools,' my father told me, and when you write of making your films in the same way you always have, of your indifference to digital tools, I understand. If those tools were good enough for Keaton and Renoir and Buñuel, they would serve for you as well. I use the dictionary I bought in London in 1964. There are better ones, but that's the one I got started on.

Such practices imply a certain care in moving through life. Things can become habitual without becoming casual. We caress them as touchstones. 'I've always been here and shall always be here,' you write of your stone house in France under the starry skies. I too revisit treasured places to show that they are still here and I am still here. Is that what brought us both back to Cannes in 2009?

On the night of your dream in 2006, you were not yet ill. In 2009, we knew of your illness, and had written messages back and forth. Sometimes you went off email for a few weeks, and I asked Nate Kohn what he had heard. Or Kyra would write me. Reading this, I know you were stunned by the horrors of chemo. I had radiation, which made it impossible for me to eat real food (at a time when I still could!) for five months. It was on my first morning at Cannes that I took my ritual dawn walk to a particular chair outside a particular cafe and ordered a *cafe au lait* and a croissant, because that was what I always ordered, and I had a breakfast for the first time since December that wasn't Ensure – chocolate, vanilla, strawberry. So I was still there. 'Madadayo,' as Kurosawa's old teacher said.

'I've always been here and shall always be here,' you write. And now you were returning to Cannes. Nate Kohn had told me you were weak. He said you insisted in speaking with his students, and said you enjoyed it. He brought you into town. We saw each other in that tent on the beach, and I am looking right now at a photo of us hugging. What wrecks we were. The chatter filled the space around us, and we sat side by side like two old soldiers, with Pierre Rissient making a third. I couldn't talk and you had no need to. I felt comfort flowing from your presence. We were there. I know now, reading these pages, how precarious your condition was at that time. How uncertain. Death was your companion. You imagined the white light at the edge of the void. And you had your old corduroy jacket and your ridiculously long scarf and you and I looked at each other and smiled – philosophically, perhaps, or bemused, at this place in life where we had washed up. Chaz was so happy to see you.

Chaz believes in dreams, and thinks there may be some healers who have gifts, and some psychics, not many, who might be able to help us. I say I don't. Yet I had one particular dream I will not describe here that came true in a very short time and in great detail. Dreams themselves in any event are real – they take place in our minds and we remember them. What they mean is hard to say. But if dreams and thoughts did not inhabit our minds, we would not know who we were, or that we are here, and would not be alive in the way we are.

I believe you consider your life as a work of art. You have political and philosophical principles and try to live according to them. You, like me, believe heath care is a human right, and we are disgusted by those who fight it on selfish grounds. You are spiritual, but not much for organised religion, and I'm with you there, except that I believe the spiritual life is all of this earth, and you leave open other possibilities. 'Fundamentalism is a hideous curse,' you write, and I agree, which is one of the reasons I admired *Salvation*. In this universe of miraculous perplexity, what wilful ignorance is required to believe one has the answers and the right to enforce them on others. Yet in Father Damien you have your saint. Chaz believes he was instrumental in your recovery. Whether he was instrumental in heaven or in your mind can be discussed, but as you absorbed the spirit of his corner of Molokai and the people he loved there, I believe something grew inside you that helped you to heal.

I suppose people read about 'meeting someone at a film festival' are think it's all a jolly glamorous convention. We've met at film festivals in Cannes, Toronto, Calcutta, Honolulu, Chicago, Urbana and who knows where else, and we were pilgrims come to perform sacraments on the altar of the cinema. Two particular memories spring up. In both of them, I was sitting next to you at screenings of one of your films. Once at Cannes we were looking at *The Human Touch* and some pig in front of us was taking calls and sending texts on his cell phone. Eventually so rewarding was this activity that he got up and left. You confided genially, 'If he hadn't left I would have pounded his bloody phone into the floor.' I wish he had stayed, so I could have witnessed the anger of the righteous.

The other screening was at Calcutta. We were looking at *Molokai: The Story of Father Damien*. Where we sat we could look directly into the open door of the projection booth and see the projectionists. The screening didn't go well. You have to help me out here. In my memory, one reel was shown upside down. Everything I know about 35mm projection suggests that is physically impossible. But it's how I remember it. The projectionists were beside themselves. What I remember from you was not anger but resigned amusement. In some larger circle of destiny, the screening was not meant to go well. You had perhaps never seen a screening go worse on purely technical grounds. It was as if you were grateful to add the experience. The man in Cannes was actively stupid. The projectionists in Calcutta were doing their best. Your film, your art, your life, were involved, but so was your sympathy.

Now I remember another screening, at Toronto. The day after 9/11, you screened *The Diaries of Vaslav Nijinsky*. I found it a work of passion, an outpouring of empathy for this troubled man. Some in the audience got up and left. Others chatted. Some were enraptured. When you stood up after for the Q&A, you were vibrating with anger. You lamented the loss of intelligent audiences and intelligent movies. You feared the best were beginning to lose all conviction The day before, we had seen the worst full of passionate intensity – the same evil that would claim the life of your friend Theo van Gogh.

But you will never lose conviction. You will never make an unworthy film. You will be a beacon. And as I read these pages, I am stunned by how well you evoke the torture of extended and extreme medical treatment. You write of the primal scream you heard at the support group. We have spoken about how people commonly praise the 'courage' of those fighting deadly disease. We agree courage has little to do with it. One does what one must. So I will not call you courageous. I will remember your speculations about the possible use of gaffer's tape in treatment. I will simply call such notions 'Paul Cox', and that will explain why it looks like courage.

Introduction by John Larkin

This is a story which should be shared: it is about the survival of one man, Paul Cox, who loved his life, then nearly lost it. A filmmaker, respected around the world for his vision and energy, describes what happened when his universe crashed and he danced with death.

The story demonstrates the resilience of the human body and spirit, the power of positive thought over fear, what is possible, even when the odds seem almost impossible, and the life-saving blessings of modern medicine.

It is about faith, too, and prayer, grace and love. It celebrates trust, and being alive.

While the story is as imaginative, deep feeling, episodic, dramatic, and inspiring as any film script, it carries the authority and authenticity of truth.

It comes in many scenes and moods. Some of them overlap as distinctions between reality and fantasy began to blur among the highly charged events and Paul's responses to them.

The tipping point, the urgent call which brought the whole story together, as Paul will relate, when the doctors and a mystery donor began to save his life and change it forever, came in the middle of the night. It is the time when the headless horseman of nameless dread can rampage and strike terror into our lonely hearts. It can also be the time when angels work best.

It was an hour well familiar to Cox, as the single-minded, self-driven artist who during a production would often work around the clock, alone in his cramped little editing room, still preferring, despite the digital age, to use his old-fashioned equipment with its tiny screen and small, scratchy speakers. Sometimes he would fall asleep for an hour or two on the floor by his workbench.

While it was often when he did some of his best work, it probably also cost him precious health.

Always on the move, he has often travelled abroad to make his pictures and see them launched at various festivals. There are frequent retrospective screenings of his work. So far he has produced forty features and documentaries, making him Australia's most prolific *auteur*.

He prefers to walk pretty well alone, apart from a small loyal band of crew and actors who support him as he struggles to make his next film on little money. Sometimes they will defer being paid, for the sake of getting the show up and running and in the can. The ensemble includes major Australian and international performers.

Cox could have gone the Hollywood way. But he has kept his distance from producers, whom he considers predatory as they dominate the industry. He is very critical of what he sees as their betrayal of a once great art, cinema, into a crude kind of consumer culture.

He has fought hard to stay independent, choosing to make films about people's inner lives, rather than the ephemeral world in which appearance is everything: the great glamour, the great illusion. His company is called Illumination Films.

The Cox collection has longevity. His major films, which continue to feature overseas and in Australia, include *Man of Flowers, My First Wife, Innocence, A Woman's Tale, Lust & Revenge, Vincent: The Life and Death of Vincent van Gogh, The Diaries of Vaslav Nijinsky, Island, Molokai: The Story of Father*

Damien and *Lonely Hearts.*

His films and his personal crusade have endeared him to a group of followers around the world.

This was evident when he became ill. Indeed, if love is the great healing force, then the degree it was projected towards him when the word went out that he was dying must surely have had something to do with his survival.

The communications became a Greek chorus to the great drama that was unfolding in Melbourne. His life has always been dramatic and risk-taking, the stuff of theatre. But this was the big one – the battle was for his life.

Cox chose the title of this story to honour Alexander Solzhenitsyn, the winner of the 1970 Nobel Prize in Literature, whose allegorical novel *The Cancer Ward* was written when he was near death with a tumour while exiled in Tashkent in the 1950s. Semi-autobiographical, it is set in a cancer therapy ward, and deals with the themes of moral responsibility, mortality and hope. These are subjects close to Cox, too.

These 'tales' were recorded by him as the events of 2009 unfolded. They have the extra value of conveying the immediacy of experience.

He does not hold back. His imagination, cries and whispers, pity, wild humour, outrage and longing for a better world, the forces which make his pictures so fanciful, heartfelt and true, are here in full flight.

In his apartment is a series of oils he painted through last year. Each shows flowers, in full bloom. One in particular reflects the entirety of his illness, leading up to his liver transplant. It is deep red. The collection was created impulsively and intuitively, without conscious intention.

Cox has always had a close personal relationship with time. He writes his scripts and makes his films quickly. He can be impatient, but also step out of time and wait for inspiration.

He has always surrounded himself with clocks, dozens of them, of all kinds and sounds, and done his own repairs. The central character in his film *Golden Braid*, a strange study in obsession based on a Guy de Maupassant story, is a clockmaker.

None of the clocks ever kept the same time, which could easily unsettle visitors. But to Cox the arrangement made sense, in his private world which is far from ordinary. He let the clocks have their own life.

In recent years, though, perhaps as an omen of what lay ahead, one by one the clocks wound down and ceased their heartbeats. The bayside Albert Park sanctuary slowly fell silent.

Now, home from hospital, we find the patient moving in slow motion around his apartment, seeking with each step a sense of place again. He is virtually in quarantine to protect his fragile immune system.

Cox previously had no time for sickness. I remember him once proclaiming that the rare times he was unwell he had no need of doctors. 'I go deep inside myself, find the darkness, and deal with it.'

We were at his ancient farmhouse retreat in the south of France, which he dreams and writes about in this book as his one true home.

The place, his *Mas*, which he has looked after for years and gradually restored, goes back to 1590. He first encountered it as a set for his Nijinsky film.

Made of stone, with endless corridors and chambers, levels and cellars, it houses a powerful spirit. It stands alone on a hill, strong and true, with the mountains in the distance. The winds come across the plains below, and the stars are close enough to put a shine on your face. From the village can be heard the church bell marking the hours, day and night. It is always rung twice, in case you did not catch it the first time. Very considerate, very French.

Cox seemed confident there, amid the solitude, the sounds of the fountain in the courtyard, nightingale songs, cries of the winds, voices within the stones, light above, and peace.

Now he is at the mercy of pills and potions, life-supporting drugs, hospital lists of dos and don'ts, and the regular monitoring of his condition. But alive.

He was always a fiery son of a Sun in Aries, but now we find him undergoing wild mood swings. One moment, he will laugh, hurting his still-raw wounds. Next, he will cry, with relief at still being alive, but also at the awful sadness that his being given life came from someone else's death.

He is vigilant and careful with his convalescence, mindful that he could still catch an infection that could finish him off. But he believes he will get through.

One of his pictures which has attracted wide acclaim is *Molokai – The Story of Father Damien*. It tells of the Belgian priest who in the late nineteenth century went and served in a little Hawaiian leper colony, where he stayed and died from the disease himself in 1889.

A former altar boy, Cox himself once began to study to become a priest. These days he finds religious dogma as difficult to swallow as a stale communion wafer. But he respects faith.

With Australian actor David Wenham playing the remarkable Father Damien, the film also featured such outstanding international actors as Peter O'Toole, Sam Neill, Leo McKern, Derek Jacobi and Kris Kristofferson.

Cox later returned to the settlement at Molokai and made a documentary, *Kalaupapa Heaven*, as his personal tribute to the residents, to whom he became very close.

It followed that when Cox himself became sick, many people prayed to Father Damien on his behalf. They believe their prayers have been answered.

They were mightily encouraged on 11 October 2009, in the midst of Paul's illness, when the Vatican granted full sainthood to Father Damien. If, as Roman Catholic tradition decrees, canonisation is possible when two after-life miracles have been proven to be directly attributable to the candidate, may it be said that the Cox survival was Father Damien's third miracle?

Back home at last from his time away in that other world, Paul's physical state is stark, but there is also something else now, a shining from within.

As a small child, he saw his neighbours die around him when the Germans invaded his home town of Venlo in the Netherlands during the Second World War. Since then, he has often struggled with feeling vulnerable. Extremely independent and private, he has had trouble accepting what other people have offered him.

Yet he could not have been more needy and exposed during his death watch, more scrutinised, publicised, talked about, open to fate. More in mortal danger, but also more blessed.

Often he thought he was going to die. For good reason. He spent 2009 living very dangerously indeed. Twice he was given mere months to live. He never felt more alone in his life.

But he told me: 'I'm fighting.' He kept sight of the light.

Needing all his energy, he could not respond very readily to others' well-meaning support, which came in waves. As Perth-based Margot Wiburd, one of his friends and colleagues, said: 'Illness seems to have its own extended family.'

One day at a time was the only course with him. No, more like one hour at a time. Or no time at all.

It was ironic that Cox would be saved in Australia. As his adopted home, where he enjoyed great earlier success with his films, he felt let him down in recent years by a reluctance to help fund his new projects.

Death has now been relegated back into the wings to await its turn again. It had come close, lurking, stalking, bringing a deep chill to the summer afternoon, a spectre as definite as it was shocking. He woke each day wondering if he was doomed.

But the head surgeon, Bob Jones, was smiling after the operation as he reported outside the theatre to the anxious Cox family: 'Paul now has a new life.'

Documentary maker David Bradbury recorded the last episodes of the operation, which altogether lasted ten hours. For his part, the patient had the best sleep in years. With the bright red cap over the top of his skull, his stately prone position and all the attention he was being given, he might perhaps have been a visiting potentate, or even, God forbid, a high priest. His hands were upturned and open, as though receiving.

His torso was wide open, revealing all the blood and guts where the surgeons had to remove the old liver and replace it with the new one, young and red and healthy.

Where did the patient go while all this was going on, the stuff of life and death, with his body undergoing such incredible change and shock?

Was he somewhere up near that sterile white ceiling among all the paraphernalia which made the theatre resemble some futuristic sci-fi set? Or, more likely, did he fly free up and out of the sealed window, away into the bright blue, high over Melbourne, across the mountains in the east, then in a cosmic wink, millions of miles out into space, dancing among the stars?

There are many other, more earthly questions, such as compatibility.

Speaking strongly and confidently through his mask, spotted with Paul's blood, Bob Jones points out that the connecting of the ends back again between the rest of the body and the incoming new organ, the meeting up and rejoining of the vascular system, takes considerable adjustment. Previously, the blood vessels belonged to two different people. Now there is only one.

As the second-largest organ after the skin, the liver is vital to life. It comes from the Anglo-Saxon word, lifer. It performs multiple functions, including detoxification, protein synthesis and the production of biochemicals needed in digestion. In the Zulu language, the word for liver (isibindi) also means 'courage'.

The liver features historically in mythology, including among several archetypes of gods and goddesses, and the occult. While seen as the source of passion, it is also synonymous with the darkest, deepest, most mysterious realm inside the human anatomy.

The first sighting of our friend at the hospital was unforgettable.

He was sitting beside his bed, wearing the ungainly hospital gown, undone at the front. There was a great slash down his belly, and a little bag of bile attached outside, almost impish, but the key to whether the new liver was working. It was bizarre to see his stomach so swollen, when the rest of his physique was refined. Fluffy white socks, hospital style, sealed his assailable appearance.

No hugs or kisses today. We all walked on feathers.

There was not much of his own world in the room. A little statue of Buddha was above the mirror on the sink opposite. His clothes were neatly folded on a chair near the bed, as though ready for immediate flight.

He had a few personal things on the tray table: leftover fruit juice, water, a small collection of Japanese poetry, and his notebook, the journal of his journey.

Those notes are the basis of this book. Postcards from hell, and heaven.

The room was small and sterile, making it impersonal.

But that did not stop the present occupant from animating it as he slowly and erratically returned to full consciousness.

The hospital staff must have found his manner, though courteous, grateful and cooperative, somewhat weird, with him, and maybe some of the morphine, doing much of the talking. For instance, the dietician, a sweet, caring young lady, seemed enchanted as Cox presented her with a long, rambling monologue on truth, love and the universe.

Other exchanges were not so playful. These we did not see: the times of new uncertainty, fear, and suffering. One night, Paul was taken back to the hospital with an infection, and screamed for hours in a pain for which there was no relief.

No one could have prepared him for some of these aftershocks. As one nurse said, in an early aside: 'It's only just started. Some people who don't know, think it [a new liver] is just like throwing a switch. It isn't ...'

As I took my leave, Paul glanced up, as though surprised. In that stillness which was beyond words, I remembered his once having said that when people come together and then part, it is the final glance that means everything.

In that last look from him, with all its intensity, the sense of his inner being was profound.

What his rebirth might do to the man and his art will be another whole story.

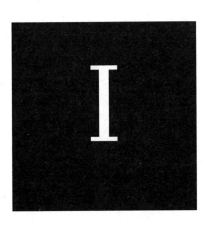

February 2009. It started one morning with a bad throbbing in my head, pain in my abdomen and a general feeling of nausea. I couldn't get myself to my feet. When my daughter Kyra arrived, she rang my doctor friend James, who paid me a quick visit. 'Better go to the hospital,' said Dr James.

Dr James Khong has been a friend for some forty years. He knows how much I dislike hospitals and conversations about health and the weather, yet he insisted I go to the Emergency Department and I remember thinking, 'I shouldn't listen to him. This is foolish.' He says now that he really had no particular reason to send me to the hospital and was surprised by his own insistence.

We didn't have to wait very long in emergency and were ushered into a cubicle, where I was offered one of those humiliating gowns that tie up at the back. A few shots of morphine later and visits to various scanning devices and we were in a solid state of confusion. Every time I returned from another mysterious trip through the hospital, the nursing staff around me had changed and new nurses would continue the endless reading of pulse and blood pressure. A young doctor came to tell me that they wanted me to stay overnight. Kyra, who'd bravely stood by, had to leave and as the night closed in I was left in Emergency with the raw sound of the wounded and the sick, in this huge factory of human misery. Next to me a Chinese family praying around the bed of a very sick woman, a bit further on, an elderly Russian man moaning and cursing. I don't think he made the morning. Later, a screaming, drunken, wounded couple accusing one another of being whores, bastards, bitches and so on, were left in front of my cubicle. They hated and cursed one another until a brave old nurse told them to shut up. That night, the whole human adventure flowed past like a dark river – the love, the betrayal, the hope, the sacrifice. Every time I dozed off, new arrivals would fill the corridors, cry or scream, or call for their loved ones. Who needs to write film scripts?

In the morning more tests, and then I'm told that there are some 'small scars' on my liver, but 'nothing serious'. In spite of the lack of sleep I feel a lot better. I phone Kyra but I'm not allowed to leave yet – one of the scans needs to be repeated. Finally, in the late afternoon, my daughter and I leave the hospital and are told that a few appointments will be made, and I will hear about results and what to do. I wanted them to whip out my gall bladder, was convinced that it was the culprit, but no such luck. I remember vaguely that somewhere along the line the word 'cancer' was mentioned, or maybe 'cancerous'. I didn't allow it to penetrate my consciousness.

I couldn't attend the first appointments because I'd accepted an invitation from the Tehran Film Festival and wanted to keep my promise. I also felt quite well again. It was good to get away from nagging thoughts and suspicions about my health, and be in a different environment. I was on the festival's jury and very much enjoyed the Iranian films that dealt with the human condition, instead of the usual violation of body and spirit one sees on the big screen.

Every morning I would have breakfast in my hotel and

read a little 'extended newssheet', *The Iran Times*. It was the thirtieth anniversary of the revolution, and each day President Ahmadinejad left a few pearls on the front page. When President Obama made some comments about 'unclenching our fists' and 'meeting up', the answer was positive. But before anything could happen Ahmadinejad insisted that Obama should apologise for George Bush. This I thought was rather original and sparked off a heated conversation among my fellow judges.

The Iranian people are warm and generous; they know about beauty and sorrow. A well-known film director told me that in spite of all the political problems he had to deal with he could never leave Iran. His cultural identity came straight from the soil of his country and was crucial to his life and his art. One wonders why and how an obsessive theocracy in an absolute minority managed to hang on to power for so many decades.

It snowed on the day I left Tehran – rather unusual I was told – and when I arrived back in Melbourne it was forty-six degrees Celsius, with ominous skies and bushfires raging not far out of town. Horrible infernos wiped whole townships off the map and many perished in the flames, including an actor we had worked with and his wife.

The first appointment back at the hospital was encouraging. There was a bit of wear and tear, but nothing too serious, and nobody paid much attention to my gall bladder. The following week I was sent to the liver clinic. The surgeon in charge was very friendly, had seen several of my early films and had a daughter who also used to work in film. He was quite honest and open and maybe a bit too casual, which meant the full impact of his words didn't really get through to me. I was too baffled. There was no eye contact, which worried me more than all the potential bad news. The doctor thought that the scarring on the liver could be cancerous, therefore it was safer to burn the spots. A small operation would just wipe them out. I thought a biopsy would still be needed and again was wondering about the gall bladder.

'If it is cancer, don't forget that cancer isn't what it used to be – enormous advances have been made. Don't worry about a thing. Your gall bladder is doing fine.'

I was quietly confused. I discussed it with Kyra, who was also quietly confused and couldn't take it too seriously. I phoned my sister, Angeline, in Holland, who was worried, but couldn't possibly think that something like cancer would befall me. I agreed with her. Apart from an infection of the heart sack many years ago, I'd always been healthy and strong. I'd always had more energy than most and only needed a few hours' sleep to rejuvenate, reinvigorate and continue on that merry road. Besides, cancer happens to other people. That's a well-known fact.

Because I worked in the arts and had admitted to drinking too much wine at times, alcohol had, according to this surgeon, played a significant part in the demise of my liver. Later they came to realise that since birth I had suffered from hemochromatosis, which is a condition where there is too much iron in the blood. I also can't deny that I gave my body a bit of a lashing at times.

I spent most of the year 2000 editing my film *The Diaries of Vaslav Nijinsky*. I drank a lot of wine, smoked many pipes and cigars, and worked endlessly behind my trusted editing machine. The whole film was shot on 35mm and although computer editing was available, I had to do it the old-fashioned way on my own, as I couldn't explain to anyone what to do with the material. The film grew as I was building the foundations – it made its own way to the silver screen. I was asked by the Toronto Film Festival to pick a date for the premiere and I wisely said, 11 September 2001. All screenings were cancelled on that fateful day. Two days later we had a small screening late at night, with Nijinsky's daughter Tamara and granddaughter Kinga there. Although it was wonderful to see the film on the big screen, the whole event was a bit of an anticlimax after three years of intense activity. Sometimes there were strange pains travelling across my abdomen, but everyone thought that I was just exhausted and should have some rest.

After the premiere and a short promotional trip through the States, I went to France and spent time walking the forests and feeling sorry for myself. A deep depression had almost paralysed me, which was much more troublesome than the pains in my abdomen. *Nijinsky* demanded much of my body and soul, and the foundations for my present condition could've been laid there.

❧❦

At my next appointment I saw a different doctor, who browsed through some of the test results and casually told me that a liver transplant would be the best. Not easy to get at my age, but there was a chance, and there were also other treatments that would be able to arrest that smouldering fire inside. There was one thing still to be done – a CAT scan of the lungs – 'just to be safe'. I'd seen pictures of cat scans and always wondered how people coped with a 'spatial journey' into 'a hole in the wall'. Kyra couldn't believe the transplant business and neither could I. She came with me when we did the scanning, and then once again there was an agonising wait until the next appointment.

Slowly, my world had changed. From the first rather casual mentioning of some small scars, I was now a marked man. There was no more doubt – no chance to escape this new status. These were not small scars. These were rather large cancerous cavities or lesions running right across my liver. 'You've got cancer of the liver,' I heard somebody say to me, and I remembered a friend, a long time ago, who went into hospital with liver problems. When I visited him, he had gone yellow, very yellow indeed, and he died soon after.

We returned to the hospital the following week. Our friend Zoe, an aspiring heart surgeon and passionate advocate of women's rights, came along for support and to interpret the technical confusions and our emotions. I knew that if the lungs were affected my chances were not the best. I tried to imagine what I would say if this were so and I was the doctor. Not an easy task.

He firstly explained about burning the spots on my liver or injecting them with localised chemotherapy. Whatever we decided now, they would test me as a candidate for a liver transplant if my lungs were all right. The CAT scan showed that my lungs were not totally clean. They revealed the presence of some nodules, and before anything could happen, in terms of a liver transplant, they had to be observed and monitored. The only way this could be done was to do another scan in three months' time. Another three months of waiting and hoping and living with great uncertainties. For now it was decided that I would return the following week to be admitted to hospital for chemo injections into the cancerous spots on my liver.

৵৽৽

These recollections were written down a few days before going into hospital, but from now on I shall try to maintain a diary of events and thoughts. There might not be a final page, but I can't let all this happen to me without doing something constructive.

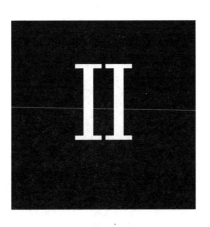

My nausea is now a constant companion, and I can't help but travel back to that fateful day when this all started. From such a casual and innocent beginning I'm now a serious cancer patient. The extent of my illness isn't really known as all cancers are different, and so are all reactions. I have been trying to unwind my clock, to find the very core of my being. To find out who I really am. Why I did the things I did. Why all and everything always mattered so much. Why the deep depressions that sometimes lasted for weeks? I tried to stop and single out one thought, one question, and meditate on that. It cleared the chaos in my mind without answering any of the questions. I did, however, realise that the peace and quiet deep inside is real and that we all have the capacity to embrace it.

I have wept alone and with my children. I have become more aware of sounds and voices beyond my immediate environment. Another dimension has been added. At first the nights were lonely and bewildering – waking up between the dreams in silent panic with a distant tram rattling by and the rain touching the roof. 'My God, help me. Hold me. I have cancer, I will die soon.' But slowly I saw my mental strength increasing. Could see that brilliant white light at the very edge of the void. That white light that becomes so much more vibrant and illuminating when it burns in the face of death. I'm calm now and try to calm down my friends and family, who have trouble coping with this sudden twist of fate.

I would like to be here a bit longer for my children – see my grandchild grow up, make another film. I have been developing a film in Europe and things were starting to look promising. A film about love and beauty and the cosmos and the organic connections between all species and organisms. I feel now fully qualified to tackle this. Meanwhile, I've taken up my still camera after some thirty years. Same camera, same light meter, same tripod. The digital revolution hasn't touched my canvas. Taking photographs I can do on my own. I don't have enough energy to deal with film and all the people who need to be considered.

❧

I have promised to give a lecture at the local arts college and writing it down, writing about the arts, has been extremely healing. I've always tried to speak my mind but now I seem to see things more clearly. Artists must protest. Start at least one revolution a day and never take anything for granted. We're living with too many contradictions, and our crazy indulgences are rarely questioned. Artists can change the world, are always changing the world. We can make a more adventurous, more spiritual, more creative society. The first step is to lose all fear and stop compromising, today in one way, tomorrow in another, by never contradicting the world around us and always following public opinion. Compromise is another word for mediocrity and failure.

Human history is the history of madness. As long as we have expensive and polluting wars on the planet, it's fairly hopeless trying to save the planet. Our civilisation has betrayed our true potential and our true spirit. We all need to protest more, to provoke more, to be more creative. Civilisations come and go. They leave their art and their history. Everything else fades in the mist of time. And from that history we learn that humankind never learned from history. I have been extremely lucky to be able to make my own films, to survive making my own films and to be able to use this medium as a means of self-expression.

છ⸱⸱⸱⸱ઉ

My latest film *Salvation* premieres in Sydney. I introduce it and answer questions. Now I'm in the plane on the way back to Melbourne. Don't feel too well, but the very thought that Kyra will pick me up with her little daughter, Arabella, cheers me up. From my window in the sky, cloud ships are hanging in midair. Below, patches of green and small yellow tracks lead towards farmhouses. The first autumn rains have already coloured the land. How forgiving and giving nature is.

I'm thinking of last night and some of the people who were there and my dear friends. Loyalty in the film world doesn't really exist except in our little circus. For some forty years we've worked together, fought together, survived together. We've all grown old and grey but the necessary fire hasn't been diminished. Filmmaking is teamwork. One needs to trust and respect the others. It is so good to see John Scott, my old editor friend; Chris Haywood, my partner in crime; Aden Young, actor and editor; Eva Sita, the actress who played a lead in *Island*; and David Wenham, who played Father Damien in *Molokai* so magically. And then there is artist and great friend

Ulli Beier, wise and wonderful at eighty-seven. It's good to have known these people, to have worked with them, loved them and remained their friend. In three days' time we will have the Melbourne premiere with other actor friends and special crew. I won't be able to attend, as I'll be in hospital having poisonous chemo injected into my liver. My brother in spirit and soul mate, Tony Llewellyn-Jones, is looking after me like an earth mother, and will introduce the film.

I've almost arrived in Melbourne – I'd forgotten about the plane. A wave of nostalgia has invaded my heart. It's hard to escape the thought of cancer and that creeping sense of loss. It's there during the day when I drink green tea instead of coffee, when I talk on the phone to friends or foes, when I write in my office or try to catch a ray of sunlight in the park. It has become my constant companion.

❧∞❦

It's Friday, and I'm going into hospital to prepare for my first chemotherapy treatment. One hears about radiation and chemo treatment for cancer patients, but I never realised what chemo does to the body – in this case, my body. The operation is terrible, with a surgeon who does his job mechanically without any warmth or sympathy towards his victim. He hurts me quite badly, but there are no words of comfort or a simple, 'Sorry, this will hurt a little.' The next ten days I spend more or less out of it. Horrible nausea, stomach pains and headaches. Sometimes I hallucinate, and animals fall from the sky. Yes, chemo might kill the cancer cells, but it also kills the healthy cells. How to build up resistance again when you've been made so ill that you cannot leave your bed? After two days I am allowed home and given notice that the procedure will have to be repeated in four weeks' time.

I can't attend the Melbourne premiere of *Salvation* because I am far too weak. Fortunately, Tony Llewellyn-Jones and actress Wendy Hughes do the introduction and answer questions.

❧

Now it's four days later and I'm still not very well. Feel miserable. I become convinced that if you have to live like this to keep yourself alive, it's better to have no treatment. I'd rather die of cancer than of chemotherapy. It's more dignified. Today they've called me in for another scan, to see if the chemo has done its lethal job. I meet a different doctor who checks me on his computer and starts arranging new appointments. As a public patient I don't have a say in the matter. There isn't much he can tell me apart from 'I'm doing fine'. I wonder about all this scanning and prodding and what's happening to the rest of my body.

❧

Have been in and out of bed, too sick to function. Now the nausea seems a little under control. I try to work my way through the letters and emails that have been flooding in and cope with a new enemy who has arrived at our doorstep. My home and office are not far from a shallow man-made waterway called Albert Park Lake. It had birch trees and old willows and a wonderful exotic bird life until some ambitious businessperson–politician managed to find enough support to ruin the park and bring the so-called Grand Prix to town. 'Men of steel, in vehicles of steel, going round and round in endless circles.' The birds flee into the sky and even my friends the magpies have gone walkabout. It's only half a kilometre from my home, and the sound of those celebrated cars is much more cruel than a dentist's drill or the saw used by surgeons to cut through the skull and get to the brain. The lunacy of speed and greed is all around me.

In the past, I wrote to newspapers and talked to those in charge. Most agreed with my points, but ignored them. 'It will put Melbourne on the map,' they said. 'Melbourne is on the map,' I used to proclaim. It's not my hometown, but I live here and thus I care. The race loses more money every year and the one argument (profits or no profits) doesn't count any more. What other good points can you think of? There are no other positive points and the 'profit line' is dubious enough. To look for profit in something so dead, so utterly desperate, is a very sick way to justify the damages, the danger and the corruption of body and spirit that comes with this sort of insanity. I wonder how many young people have been killed throughout the years, imitating the power of speed and the glamorisation of the motorcar? The sound of a speeding Formula One vehicle itself tells us that we're dealing with something unnatural, something totally out of tune with our capacity to hear, think, digest, store and remember. One night at the hospital, a sick old woman had fallen asleep whilst her TV set was still on. The Grand Prix, interrupted by silly commercials, was playing loudly to the annoyance of some other patients. The nurses were busy, so I took it upon myself, to turn the sound down.

The woman woke up immediately and said, 'I had a terrible dream, somebody was trying to make a hole in my brain'.

As I write, the sound of the practising jets overhead becomes so vile and destructive that I ask Wendy Hughes to drive me to the country. Wendy is my comrade and much loved performer in many of our films. It's a strange day with sudden splashes of rain and bursts of intense sunlight. We're such old friends and don't need to say very much. I can feel that Wendy is worried about me but then she tells me that I'm going to be fine and that all this will pass. We talk and laugh about her mother who died of cancer some thirty years ago. She loved playing the pokies and often nursed a 'tennis elbow' from working the slot machines for too long. We arrive at an old beautiful farmhouse where John Larkin and Dawn Davis have settled. We're all pleased to see one another and walk with Dawn to check her newly planted trees.

After Wendy has left I find myself lying on a make shift bed on the veranda, out of the way from all violation and noise of the world. Here you can see the Milky Way and all the stars of the universe.

I must be thankful to the two jets that made me flee. They didn't know that I'm a war child, that during the war we often emerged from our shelters and found everything destroyed – dead bodies lying in the ruins and people digging through the stones to find their loved ones. For the first five years of my life I saw nothing but death and destruction. As I wrote in my autobiography, *Reflections*, 'We were always pleased and amazed to find our house still standing after a bombardment and the people we loved alive. Many, however, perished in the ruins and the flames. Still today, whenever I see and hear more than one plane in the sky I feel hurt and ill at ease. "I am in danger, I must hide." As a four-year-old I saw the sky suddenly darken and the light disappear when hundreds of planes flying close together obscured the light.' The Grand Prix planes, celebrating the event from above, remind me too much of that horror. What has the Grand Prix to do with cancer, one may ask? I think the Grand Prix is a cancer. A greedy modern cancer – deadly and dangerous.

Early sun dances across the wooden floor. Apart from a few birds, this world is still – so very still. I can't comb my hair any more – even my hair hurts. I try to put it in some sort of shape or order, but it doesn't stay and wanders away from my head. People lose their hair through chemotherapy. I am lucky, mine is all there, looking wild and dishevelled.

This place in the country has a beautiful view, or rather many beautiful views, across the distant mountains. Don't know what mountains they are, but in the glowing early morning sunlight these mountains are alive and shape the intensity of my thoughts and feelings. Two red parrots take a bath in a little fountain. Everything has ceased to exist for them and even for me. Splashing in the water is a 'total activity'. Nothing else matters. Then there's a rose garden that Rimbaud would've treasured, and a hanging garden leading towards a statue of Buddha. When the rains return (will they ever come back?) this place will be the most beautiful paradise. My friends travel 150 kilometres to get to town to do their jobs, yet it's worth all the driving and the chaos. To return at night to the stars and hear nothing but a few night birds is such a luxury. It's unnatural to live in the cities and switch off the stars. John and Dawn are at ease here and make me feel at home. We're quiet, almost silent in tune with one another's inner thoughts.

John drives me all the way back, kind giant of a man. When we arrive in town, the madness has come to a grinding halt and a sense of so-called normality is about to return to the city. John gets back on the road before the hoons hit the highway; they probably would force him off the road if he didn't break the speed limit to stay away from them.

ॐ

This morning we go to see another doctor. This doctor has a sense of humour. He is not as knowledgeable as the experts but more human. It's humanity, warmth and tenderness I need more than expert advice at this point. Kyra is there again at my side. Brave and as bewildered as I am. So very good to have her fighting the good fight with me. Although there is nothing uplifting to report, it is good to see this man. He makes me feel part of the human species. Makes me forget that I'm a marked man.

In the afternoon we discuss what to ask the surgeons at the hospital. Tomorrow morning we have another appointment and maybe will discover a little more about nodules and polyps, chemo and CAT scans and whatever other new words have entered my fragile new world.

Kyra, my child, my comrade in arms. Often I took her with me on my travels, didn't want to leave her behind. We somehow managed the world. I felt secure with her. Her headmaster warned me that nothing would come of this girl, who spent too much time out of school, but I couldn't leave her behind and she loved exploring new worlds. She always carried her large collection of small bears with her. A special suitcase had been organised to accommodate the bears, but the lock wasn't very solid. One day, on the tarmac in Edmonton, Canada, her bears rebelled and escaped en masse from the suitcase. Together with the stewardess and a passing pilot we managed to round up the bears and return them to Kyra's travelling home.

Somehow Kyra and I grew up together. She was about five when she came to live with me permanently. Instead of my apartment, I managed to secure a house for us with a large garden and much space and tranquillity. I learned how to cook and how to use a hot iron! It was a good home for the two of us – until my financial situation collapsed and the house had to be sold in a hurry.

☙❧

There's no escape from the repeat chemo treatment. Again they will invade my body through the groin and travel towards the liver. I'm told what is going to happen. There's no discussion. At some point it's better to surrender and trust. Everybody seems to know more than I do. This is the third different surgeon I've dealt with. I'm a public patient and have to wait my turn and fit into the system. That's all right with me. Education and health should always be the same for everyone if we want to live in a fair and just society. How can there ever be any arguments about this? Lots of things, for instance, are wrong with Cuba, but education and health there are the same for all. The people are not rich in body but certainly in spirit. It's a marvellous country to visit.

Life isn't merely for living, but what we live for. It's not easy to give form and shape to those darker forces that linger inside, but even the smallest attempt gives purpose to the creator and might help others to see more openly. When one is confused or depressed one should create something – make or do something that wasn't there before. It is most healing for the spirit and helps one to find one's way again in the chaos. Despite the impression some people have of me as an artist of dubious merit, I've always been a responsible member of our so-called society, paid my taxes and my bills and tried to teach my children to be responsible and enjoy the art of giving rather than the art of taking. And if I had taken my initial popularity and success to Hollywood, I could've made much money and would now be able to pay for private cancer treatment and maybe even invest in a liver or two.

It alarms and saddens me that our civilisation celebrates greed and ignorance. Too many people who have talents use them to make money, more money, without realising that these gifts belong to our fellow man and not to our bank managers. What a ludicrous world of compromise – today in this way, tomorrow in another – always on the freeway to mediocrity. Through my newly acquired vulnerability and raw emotional state, I meet and respond to people on a totally different level. I'm much more alert to the uniqueness of a single smile, a single touch. An image, a tender memory or an act of kindness can bring instant tears to my eyes. At first this threw me – now it strengthens me, gives me a degree of judgement and clarity I didn't have before.

In his beautiful *De Profundis*, Oscar Wilde wrote, 'When I get out of prison, the only people I would care to be with are artists and people who have suffered. Those who know what beauty is and those who know what sorrow is'. Yes indeed. When I get out of this prison …

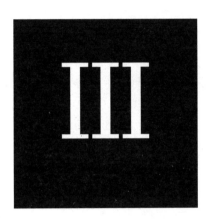

3 April 2009. I haven't worried about dates for many months. Then, just recently, across the top of the front page of Australia's leading newspaper, I encountered a gaunt picture of myself on a red background with the heading – 'Paul Cox, on life, films and cancer news'. It's a disgusting act of betrayal. A journalist had been told to ask me if I minded talking about my cancer while being interviewed about *Salvation*. I casually said, 'I have nothing to hide.' Her interview was quite sensitive and respectful, but one of the paper's editors must have thought that the cancer announcement was good news and would present a new twist to my glorious career. The basic message, and one that would be taken up by other media, is that I am probably dying. Soon after this 'Act of Betrayal' I am bombarded with letters, emails and phone calls. Some people in tears. 'Why didn't you tell me?' I spent days comforting shocked friends and even strangers. I do not have the energy to cheer up the world around me.

Although it's sixteen days since the chemo snake was pushed through my arteries, I still haven't fully recovered. I had never been told that this would be such an ordeal, nor that there was more to come. In ten days I shall once again face this poisonous attack on my organic being. Everybody says this is the right thing to do. Who knows what is the right thing to do? One thing I know for sure is that I will once again suffer the horrible consequences.

Suddenly, I have time but no energy. I used to have no time but lots of energy. There's not much money left in my system here, but enough to survive. Money has never been high on the list. Too easy to spend, too easy to make if one concentrates on it. The real God among Man is money. It floods the Earth disguised as currencies, various currencies that change in value according to a few who benefit from it. Everybody wants money – yet in essence nobody controls it. The people who accumulate lots of money are celebrated, admired and respected, even though often they've acquired it by means of deception and dishonesty. People who have been blessed with talent too often spend it on making money instead of using it to help their fellow man. Spending money is called a healthy economy – spending is called sharing and investing wealth. The healthier the economy, the less humanity is being shared. People kill for money, go to jail for money, are prepared to lose all they love for the sake of money. Money is power – power corrupts – corruption is money. Money is another cancer among us. Probably the most deadly, the most dangerous, the most disgusting cancer that eats the soul and often turns Man into the lowest and most disgusting creature on Earth.

છૠૐ

The chemo clouds are slowly leaving me. I have been ill for a long time. Strangely enough, I didn't dream. No dreams at all. Last night my dream world returned with a vengeance. Frantically I tried to write it all down, but already lost too much.

A smoky room near a railway line. Two small film crews

are waiting for lunch. A woman is taking orders. We're here to film a funeral. Someone has died. We don't know who it is. A producer with a thick Russian accent tells me we need a surprise element to entice the viewers. I spot my friend and fellow filmmaker Werner Herzog sitting near a window. Large trains go past so close that the front wall of the room becomes a train but we're not moving with it. Werner doesn't know who's died either. We've both been asked to film the event and agree that the person who died was important to the film world in general and to us in particular. Then we realise that we don't know whom we're talking about. I feel that it could be one of us, but it must be Werner, because how could I tell the story if I were dead? But I can see in Werner's eyes that he thinks I'm dead. Somehow we have to see this through together. Meanwhile the two film crews are still waiting for lunch. They all look vaguely familiar. I scream a little too loudly at the lady who's supposed to get lunch for the crew. Realise I'm a bit over the top because I want to prove I'm alive. Outside in the street my old Mercedes arrives driving backwards. There's nobody inside. The car looks a bit like a hearse. Then we're finding ourselves walking behind the coffin. Werner is quite stoic. He doesn't think it's very important who is in the coffin. We're both ridiculously dressed in black outfits with large hats. We're actually more embarrassed about looking like that than our confusion about the dead body. By now we're holding hands, both aware that there're dark demons at work here. We're walking into a cemetery. There's a brass band. People are singing, some are dancing. Stone Age figures moving between the trees, becoming trees then human figures again. A choir is singing. All are crying. Large tears that form a small creek running towards the grave site. The tension increases. Who's dead? Werner, me or somebody else? One thing has become very clear. Does it really matter? Life and death are given to us to become richer in spirit. Time creates a sense of reality, but the truth lies in timelessness. The God within is creation – outside of that there's no God. If one of us dies, he has to die within himself, not outside of himself. All of this is terribly clear to me. As I write this, dark clouds are beginning to move into my mind. I have to be quick.

Then I think – how can I see and understand all that if I'm dead? People I've known and loved, dead and alive, appear. From my late soul brother Norman Kaye to the butcher's son who sat next to me in first grade. He had aged accordingly. Then we arrive at the gravesite and to my great surprise, Roger Ebert is standing behind a microphone to give a speech. This is not possible. Roger has lost his voice, how can he speak now? It flashes though my head that he has regained control, not through an operation, but through a divine miracle or blessing. Werner looks at me. Is Roger also on the list? But how can I see and dream all this if it's me? Werner reassures me once again that it doesn't matter. The dream is now so real I feel this can't be a dream any longer. Everybody is here. There are two other American friends, Chaz and Nate, with their children. Pam, Nate's wife, is standing at a distance. Dusty Cohl, wearing a white hat, and his wife Joan, producer Hannah Fischer, my friend Oliver from the office, Tony Llewellyn-Jones, my four sisters dressed in yellow and pink. Joanie and Jim Currie, my sound designer and friend for many years, with a huge microphone. I miss my children, but I'm also glad they're not around. Everyone around the gravesite, the dead and the living feel a deeper awareness, deeper reality. We all travelled a long distance to embrace this 'dearly beloved'. Even if it's me in the coffin, what's the big deal? I'm surrounded by warmth and a glowing feeling of hope. Roger starts to speak, his voice croaks. Wish I could remember now what he said. All of us dissolve into the earth, even the grave disappears.

Easter 2009. Mild sunny days with little traffic or agitation in the street. People have left the city and are having their Easter dinners in various country homes. I feel distressed and deserted, although there is great warmth and love around me. A dear friend has come all the way from London to be with me for a few weeks. She's a generous and caring soul. It's a new experience to have another human being physically close to you – next to you at night and waking with you in the morning. As Vincent van Gogh wrote, 'When you wake up in the morning and find yourself not alone, but see there a fellow creature beside you, it makes the world look so much more friendly. Much more friendly than religious deities and whitewashed church walls'.

Meanwhile, I'm preparing myself for the next chemo treatment. Tomorrow is my sixty-ninth birthday. Can't help thinking, 'Will there be a seventieth birthday?' Every day is a lifetime; every hour is a lifetime and every minute and second is a lifetime. To live another ten years would be good, but one must have the strength to give and create, to prepare some gifts. If not, there's little point in prolonging life on this Earth. Tomorrow also, a new digital print of an earlier film, *My First Wife*, will be screened. I'm looking forward to seeing it on the big screen. The film was made under much pressure at a time in my life when dramatic changes were imminent.

16 April. Sixty-nine today. When you're young, this age

seems ancient. But I haven't aged the way I probably should have. Still feel about forty and behave accordingly. So far, age has never troubled me. I'd like to live a few more years because I haven't come to the end of the road yet. So many pathways still to be explored. What to do with so many possibilities? I am back staring at the whitewashed walls of my cancer ward. I'm ready for my second chemo treatment. Waiting to be wheeled into the operating theatre. Everybody wants to know what I'm writing. Nothing earth shattering, I say, just trying to keep an account of events.

This is a three-hour operation with much more care and respect than the first shot of chemo. Through the various tubes I see a screen with my main artery exposed like the origins of a riverbed. Inside our bodies we have the same organic shapes as those we find in nature or in the universe. Everything is connected; everything belongs to one large organism. A long tube is pushed through the artery towards the liver. I can't follow it any further because the picture disappears behind some obstacles, and a strong nausea makes it difficult to keep my eyes open. But I see part of the universe within my own body. Sleep a few hours in the ward until the so-called evening meal appears. Chemo also affects the memory bank, and a degree of delayed vision is certainly affecting me. I always remember my dreams, but usually let them go if there's nothing of interest that lingers. Now I know that I had a dream, but there's nothing left of it in my conscious or subconscious mind when I wake.

22 April. After two days in hospital, I come home and now look at the world from my own bed. My point of view counts again. I am a person! It's very early in the morning. In the

distance the threatening sounds of the city. I've always been lucky and never 'travelled to work'. Either I lived above my office or lived in so many different places or countries that needed to be explored and understood before there was any routine established. This ominous sound can only be stopped by closing the window. And I feel it should be stopped. With the sound comes a threat, a reminder of useless duties. Our society has made a mockery of what it means to be an individual. We're not end products of our society. We're used, manipulated and abused as so-called individuals. It celebrates the exterior without acknowledging the interior, and thus a healthy interaction between the inner and outer is totally ignored and not possible. Some people spend a lifetime in a job they don't like, living a life they don't want, and the money they earn is spent on things they don't need. Usually more money than they earn.

The chemo clouds have allowed me a little breathing time, even though they are hiding me away from the world of reason. If I ever were to conquer my imminent demise and find myself with a few more years, I would live in the country in France. I would spend my time staring at the Cévennes Mountains from my kitchen window and live a life of peace and quiet with the right rhythm and simple fresh food every day. I will go there soon, to this ancient old farm that I stumbled across a long time ago.

There're so many things I want to write about but the mind wanders, leading to little concentration and hardly any words. Tomorrow I'll be put through some scanning device to see if the chemo has worked any better than last time. Feel sick, lost and deserted. A hopeless day of too many mixed emotions and thoughts of self-pity. As I say to others who tend to cry over me – your tears are of no use to me. So I must tell myself, 'Your emotional upheavals and self-indulgences are of no use to me.' We can't be on top of it all the time and be strong. Of course it's good to let go for a moment and flow with that last fear – that fear of losing your very life.

❧

The days have flown past ... not much to report ... not much to write. I try to live a pure life, eat the right food and do all the right things. The chemo nausea still hasn't settled. We've been told that the chemo hit its target and this time it worked. I have no way of judging this.

I'm now being treated in two hospitals. Liver transplants are being performed in the second hospital, and the doctor and nurses explain to me what's required. A tiny bit of light shines in the dark. I'm still being considered for liver transplantation, if I pass all the other tests. It's not much but after some four months where things grew darker all the time, and never a glimmer of light appeared from anywhere, it's something to almost celebrate. Wendy Hughes offers to drive me to the new hospital for an appointment. We get a bit lost on the way to the other side of town and then get lost again in the labyrinth of corridors at the hospital.

We finally find the doctor, a kind man, who has a sense of humour. Wendy observes the proceedings quietly and listens carefully to our conversation. Then she suddenly interrupts and asks the doctor how much time I've got left. She looks surprised about her own question. The doctor says it is hard to assess, but wants to be frank and honest and thinks probably some six months. It is longer than I suspected and I feel quite pleased, but dear Wendy is shocked and remains touched and tearful as we make our way back to the other side of town.

Now a lot of the tests have to be repeated because the new hospital will probably take over. All that blood moving from one tube to the next. How much blood? Where did it come from? How long has it been with me? Are they going to throw it out after the tests have been completed? Is this blood contaminated? Who has my blood?

I've been trying to tell the doctors that I need to go and see my family. I need to spend some time with people of my own blood. I simply need to be in Europe. All my life I've been homesick but never really knew where home is or was. This wave of nostalgia tells me it's somewhere in Europe. Now I want to feel the French soil under my feet, see the sunflowers and the poppies and the stunning glow over the mountains when the sun sets. I want to walk through the ancient forest outside of my town in Holland and smell the 600-year-old bark that covers the trees like an iron harness. Then I want to stand in front of Vincent van Gogh's self-portrait at the Kröller-Müller Museum and thank Vincent for all the joy and beauty he brought into my life. And maybe visit the greatest master of them all, the modest genius Johannes Vermeer, who showed us the universe by painting his own backyard.

When I grew up there was a birthday calendar with Vincent's reproductions on the toilet door. It was there for many years, with new names being added and some being crossed out. Every month a new picture could be viewed from the safety of the toilet seat. My mother liked the *Sunflowers* the best. They featured in my birth month, April. She would tell me about Vincent and why he was such a special painter. Forty years later I would make the film *Vincent – The Life and Death of Vincent van Gogh*.

Dear Vincent … ten years of creation, agony and elation.

But his power has not faded – his yellow is even more yellow, his passion even more passionate. How lucky I am to have been introduced to him at an early stage. To have lived with him, his words and his thoughts, to have been compelled to make his film. After some thirty years, all those who worked on the film are still deeply affected – from the great painter Asher Bilu, who art directed, to John Hurt, who became Vincent's voice and was crucial to the success of the film. When *Vincent* screened at the Toronto Film Festival, an admiring fan with a sunflower chased me – I just managed to get into a lift and escape her clutches. A bemused gentleman in the lift introduced himself: Theo van Gogh, the great grandson of Vincent's brother Theo. We went up to the top floor, shared a drink, talked about film, and became friends for life. For the next twenty-five years, Theo was always there at the end of the phone or waiting for me whenever I got back to Holland. He was developing himself as a fine filmmaker in his own right, and our conversations were stimulating and electric. Often we walked around a large park in Arnhem without saying a word, and came home rejuvenated.

Theo was a sharp and witty writer, and his TV interviews of politicians and people of relevance and irrelevance were extremely interesting and revealing. Few would've realised that Theo was a true romantic. One day he suggested that we should make a film about love, in two parts. Each would direct one part and the script would be written together with my comrade Judith Herzberg, a poet and a writer of great warmth and imagination – a national icon in Holland, and a wonderful human soul. She and I had met years before when we were invited to co-write a screenplay. We liked working together but our efforts weren't much appreciated by the producers. After a few weeks we were fired by a little man who called himself 'the producer'. This brought enormous relief for both of us. Judith is a poet and although she loves the medium of film can't stand the 'bums on seats mentality'.

I asked Theo to go and see Judith. He had made some comments in the press that sounded rather anti-Semitic, and Judith wasn't at all sure about him. Theo raged against all and everything when he felt a little rebellious. Ridiculous as it sounds, it also helped him to hide his tenderness and his true romantic self. He visited Judith with a stack of his films under his arm, and told me later that when he had rung the bell, he almost fled her house due to nervousness.

The last time I saw Theo was four days before his death. He came at night from a meeting in Belgium and had been in a confrontation with some Muslim fundamentalists. It had been more serious than he admitted. Theo was a compulsive agitator. Couldn't help himself. He fiercely defended the truth, as he perceived it at a particular time. He was also the most generous, loving, passionate friend I've ever had. Extremely intelligent and extremely generous. When we parted I said, 'Please be careful, Theo – keep your mouth shut if possible. Those people are dangerous.' Theo, looking like a naughty schoolboy, laughed and said, 'Who would ever want to harm the village fool.' At the time he was on a mission against Islam and raged against fundamentalism and the lack of criticism Islam received in Holland.

I left for Australia the day after, and when I arrived, there were many disturbing messages on my answering machine. Something had happened to Theo, but no one said what had happened. Only when I rang my sister, I learned that this very special man had been brutally murdered on the streets of Amsterdam. Later I saw a photograph of Theo lying spread-eagled in the street, with a dagger stuck into his warm and wonderful human heart.

Fundamentalism is a hideous curse. Nothing was achieved by murdering Theo, except that Holland lost one of its most colourful and interesting people. As his producer friend Gijs van de Westerlaken said, 'Holland has become a dull place without Theo.' It's five years since that fateful day. I still think of him every day.

❧

We're about to land in Amsterdam. A golden morning light touches the land. This is the country of my birth, although I never truly felt at home here. Some thirty years ago, when we started to work on *Vincent – The Life and Death of Vincent van Gogh*, I felt a similar flood of emotion. When the plane landed, I felt for the very first time that I'd come home; that even I belonged. Now I land with a heart full of conflicting emotions. I feel moved for very different reasons. My sister Angeline, with her husband, Jaap, and my brother, Wim, have come to pick me up. It was only after I'd gone to Australia that we started to become truly connected. What a relief it is to hold them, to kiss them, to walk with them. During our youth we never got to know one another very well.

❧

For almost a week I sit quietly in the house that was an exchange for our family home. At the back, tall trees and some white blossoms and young green sprouting from every corner. The many shades of green are so thick that it feels and looks as if one is in the country. The house is a bit like a museum, with bits and pieces from every country on Earth. I'm a compulsive junk collector and have filled every corner and empty wall with reminders of my travels and the people I've met. I'm trying to put a bit of order in all the chaos.

I've been strangely optimistic in the last few days. There's not much reason to be, but it's certainly better than feeling fear and confusion. I've also spoken to a woman who had a liver transplant some seven years ago. Her need for transplant wasn't due to cancer. A misconception of mine – I thought it was mostly related to cancer, but it rarely is. Usually hepatitis B or C is the culprit.

14 May. And now I'm in the south of France, in this beautiful old farm at the edge of the small village of Rivières de Theyrargues. A great stillness has engulfed this land. There are layers of stars in the sky, a three-dimensional *Starry Night*. Millions and millions of stars upon stars. I've never seen a sky like this. Even though my life is fading, I feel connected – have always been connected. I've always been here and shall always be here. Then – in that vast universe and that immense silence – a nightingale starts to sing, and love and beauty and tenderness grow as large as all the galaxies in the sky. It is wonderful to be in the country: this is how we should live and relate to the earth. What bliss it is to look at the mountains and sit in the sun. If I recover from this ordeal, I intend to live here. Fill my days with simple tasks and maybe venture out

one more time to make a film. I'm now fully qualified to film the human condition in one way or another and spend more time on detail. It's the small things in life that matter and add up to the big picture. Officially, I have three and a half months left to live. Instead of accepting this as my present truth, I will fight the good fight and extend my stay on this Earth. What is this force that makes us cling to life and refuse to accept our mortality?

Tomorrow I will leave for Cannes. As the horrible saying goes, 'the show must go on'. There're a few meetings planned and other people to talk to. Also I will give a lecture to students of the University of Georgia. I will tell them about anarchy and the duty of the artist. About giving rather than taking, about the creation and awareness of beauty, rather than being consumer-conscious and following the trend of the day, and consequently always moving towards mediocrity. I try to keep the show on the road by attending a few meetings about my scripts *Centre of Gravity* and *Homecoming*, which were planned some time ago, and discussing future plans with various old friends and foes.

I meet with Roger and Chaz Ebert and Nate Kohn. Roger is honoured with some award. We try to share a few jokes and communicate, but there isn't much space and time for two old soldiers crippled by a horrible disease. I also feel most uncomfortable sitting in front of strangers, who watch us caged animals from behind their drinks and nibbles. I've just read Roger's concept about God, death and the universe. A brilliant essay using Vincent van Gogh's writing as a metaphor. The exterior is always deceptive. Roger's body is so badly wounded and his voice has been silenced, but his writings are deep and profound and full of poetry.

I've had confrontations with quite a few healers in the last few months. So many well-meaning people recommend someone, make contact with people who have the secret key to the universe and the healing powers of the Earth. I intend to exhaust conventional methods first, and then maybe work my way through the many voices that promise salvation. My brother so much wants to help me and speaks to a healer who comes highly recommended. The healer had never met me – never knew I existed. I am the brother of the man who phones him and asks for help. The man tells my brother that something happened to me when I was fourteen or fifteen – I should try to remember. Oh dear, what could that be? It could've been around the time that I discovered that girls also grew pubic hair, which indeed shook the foundations of my little universe, but left no lasting scars! Next thing he's so convinced that he can help that he has already posted a box with goodies to my brother for the meagre sum of €500. Also, a time for a special consultation should be organised, for a special price. Other personal info was following.

What am I to think of all this? We're not dealing with someone whose car has broken down and is not sure what replacement parts are needed to fix the vehicle. We're dealing with a vulnerable man who's fighting for his life. If I wanted to help him as a fellow human being, I certainly wouldn't pressure him with expensive healing components. This healer knows that I follow conventional treatment first before throwing myself to the wolves, but claims that I should already mix this with his methods so that I'll be ready for his fangs when the time comes. There are many of these people lurking around. I'd like to know everything about this man – his so-called success rate – why he dares to charge a large amount of money for all sorts of substances without having discussed this or explained the benefits. There's something sinister, extremely sinister, about such people.

Since the news of my condition became known, a remarkable group of charlatans has gathered around with cures that promise Eternal Life. All that's required is a healthy bank account and a proper disease that makes one a little scared to face the world and too vulnerable to make rational decisions. There will be, of course, among all these people, some noble souls with noble intentions and a true ability to heal or help. They certainly wouldn't charge €500 up-front and talk about a so-called traumatic experience that happened some fifty years ago.

I'm back in Arnhem, slowly preparing myself for my return to Australia. They are going to do all the tests there that are needed for me to be accepted for the transplant list. Family and friends come to visit. I find it difficult to respond to them, even though my heart screams out. I need to be on my own most of the time. I don't want anyone to cry out over me or tell me how much they care and love me. I need to protect my feelings, my strength. If I let myself go, I won't survive emotionally and consequently physically. Anyone who thinks and feels and struggles, knows how important it is to balance or at least make an attempt at balancing the inner and the outer, to achieve a degree of completeness as a human being. It's hard to keep that up when my exterior is disintegrating. In a few days I will leave this house. Trying to put everything in order seems to be the right thing to do, although there's not much chance that I will see this house again.

It's a major problem to try to go to sleep. Not because I'm afraid or feel lonely or worried about what's in store. I've never been a good sleeper, and this has gotten worse as time has gone by, and every time I think I'm going to slip into the safety of the night, something happens in my brain – I become bewildered by a memory that remains small, but gathers significance as it explores me.

❧

They've accepted me for a week of tests to see if I'm transplant material – that there's not more cancer lurking in my bones and that I'm physically and mentally strong enough to survive a ten-hour operation. I know I'm strong enough – I know I can and will survive if they give me the chance to face these tests. I'm returning to Australia two weeks early because it looks like I will be given this chance. At least we will find out if the cancer has spread, and if it has, I will know how to take my leave. It must happen with dignity and hopefully a smile. I feel as if my body no longer belongs to me. Maybe I never belonged to my body either. My European visit has moved quickly. Tomorrow I will return to Australia and face reality.

❧

Angeline and Jaap have been a great comfort. Tonight we sit in silence and share a meal. Tomorrow they will travel with me to Amsterdam. I would prefer them to stay here and let me disappear quietly. But they are my real family. Throughout the years of separation, living on either side of the world we've grown very close. We never have an argument or disagreement. We simply agree! Angeline has a big golden heart. Never had children, but looks after everyone and anyone with the generosity of an earth mother. She was there to give our mother some joy in her final years, and looked after our father until his final breath. Meanwhile she lives a busy life, lecturing in the arts, organising exhibitions and trying to find time for her own delicate paintings and drawings. We part, of course, in tears. They stand there a long time after I'd gone through Customs. I watch them, hidden in the crowd.

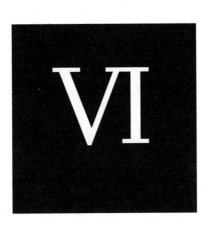

Fourteen hours to get to Singapore. I fall asleep in my business-class cocoon. What a luxury. An American sponsor made it all possible. In the United States they say, 'We love your work – what can we do for you? How can we help?' In Australia it's more like 'Love your work – good for you!' I don't expect support or special treatment. Nobody is more special or deserves more than the other. The thing I expect, though, is human warmth, a degree of trust and respect and the security of knowing that we're all doing our best and always try to help those who are in need of help. It's cold and wet in Melbourne. Still don't understand why this became my hometown. I think the creative indifference of the place allowed me to concentrate and develop my work. In all those years I rarely ventured out or mixed with the outside world. Only with a few close friends and during productions would I be inclined to be social. It's different when I'm in Europe or North America. Yet here I have many friends and many people care. Tomorrow I'm in for a bone scan at the nuclear medicine department. I've heard that all hell will break loose if you try to go through the scanners at the airport afterwards. I will be a nuclear time bomb for a few days. And next week the final tests to determine whether I'm eligible for a liver transplant. If I'm not, there's not much I can do, but at least I know where I stand and which of the many demons that lurk in the dark are to be confronted. I'm facing a labyrinth of contradictions, inside myself and outside. Twice I've been told how much time is left. Both times came and went – I'm still here, feeling quite strong and well. I'd surrendered to the idea of dying soon and felt quite at peace with the very thought. Now I feel the opposite. I'm rewriting my script *Centre of Gravity* and want to live, want to create – finish the many ideas that circle around my feeble brain. I don't understand this sudden flutter of hope. Nothing tells me I have a future. But I realise more than ever that I've been cursed or blessed with a creative urge that still rages, even in the face of death.

From a very kind and knowledgeable doctor, whom I visited in Holland, I received a proper evaluation of my condition. Looks pretty grim, but at least I know the reality. Also now I don't have to explain to others what is going on. I have found that extremely frustrating. Questions, questions to which I have no proper answers or get so confused that I give different answers to different people. Here's the letter, which makes it easier to understand the situation.

Dear Mr. Cox

I have discussed your case with two radiologists, a transplant surgeon and a hepatologist. There is a variety of opinions. I have tried to formulate a conclusion, and I will point out what the difficulties/areas of uncertainty are.

First conclusion is that there is cirrhosis of the liver – that is, scarring due to chronic damage, with changes of the normal liver architecture. The function of the liver still is good (mildly disturbed): that is not a problem. It is still to be determined what the cause of the liver disease is. Alcohol has been mentioned: most of us (including the hepatologists) drink more than hepatologists deem wise. I may be wrong, but I do not regard you to be an 'alcoholic'. There is suspicion that there is increased iron deposition in your body: this might be due to hemochromatosis, an inherited disease in which the body absorbs too much iron that is deposited in the liver and other organs (e.g., the heart, the pancreas, joints) and may damage them. Importantly, amounts of alcohol that are not too worrisome by themselves may become harmful in combination with iron excess. So it is important to know whether iron plays a role. There is a number of ways to get this information: blood tests, a liver biopsy or an MRI scan of the liver (hopefully the lipiodol that was given during chemoembolisation gives no disturbance of the measurements). If iron would play a role, it is of course necessary whether the liver is the only victim or that other organs are affected as well.

Second conclusion is that there are several lesions in the liver. In a cirrhotic liver, a nodule always raises the suspicion of liver cancer (hepatocellular carcinoma, HCC for short). HCC is not the only possibility, because a cirrhotic liver becomes nodular, and many nodules are not malignant. There are several ways to determine the nature of a lesion: the pattern of contrast enhancement in a scan, tumor marker(s) in the blood, a biopsy, or changes over time (if it does not grow, chance of malignancy is very very low). In your case, the lesions showed contrast uptake early (which is consistent with liver cells in the lesion, either benign or malignant), but according to our most experienced liver radiologist, the lesions did not show early washout of contrast (which is typically seen in HCC but not in benign lesions). Tumor markers were negative (which does not exclude HCC). There was strong uptake of lipiodol however. Taken together, the most likely diagnosis is HCC, although this is not 100% certain.

Third conclusion is more difficult: the number of lesions. The most experienced radiologist described 2 lesions, both about 3 cm in diameter, with no change between the CT scans of Jan and March this year. The second radiologist thought that there might be more lesions (one of the lesions might consist of two lesions next to each other – these were described as separate lesions by the Australian radiologist as well – and there might be 2 additional lesions. I am not fully convinced of the latter, as this conclusion was based on the CT scan after lipiodol, which is difficult to interpret.

Cirrhotic livers are inhomogeneous, and are notably difficult to judge on imaging. Your liver is not different in that regard.

Fourth conclusion is about potential spread outside the liver. There are a couple of small nodules in the lungs, which are judged as non-suspect for tumor. I hope that the follow-up scan confirms that. Lymph nodes in the abdomen are difficult to interpret, and are often present in patients with liver disease. Follow-up scans will tell us more, but at this time these do not worry us too much.

Fifth conclusion again is difficult. However, based on my strong suspicion of HCC, my advice would be transplantation. Chemoembolisation is not a curative treatment. Resection of part of the liver is difficult: probably, the capacity of your liver would not be sufficient to tolerate that, and moreover, HCC in cirrhotic liver is often present at more spots (or will develop elsewhere in the liver). This is of course a problem with all types of local treatment: only what is recognised as abnormal is treated.

There are a couple of provisos regarding transplantation. One would have to be as certain as possible about the diagnosis. Perhaps MRI scanning might be helpful (that is, if the lipiodol does not disturb the imaging). Disease should not be demonstrable outside of the liver (lungs, lymph nodes), because it would make transplantation futile. The extent of tumor in the liver is another point. As told, Eurotransplant follows the Milano criteria. That is, HCC is acceptable as an indication if there is 1 lesion of max 5 cm in diameter, or at most 3 lesions, with the largest max 3 cm in diameter. I do not know whether the Australian centers follow these same criteria or are more liberal. Naturally, a patient should be physically and mentally healthy and able to undergo major surgery.

Ideally, a transplant should be done at short notice in order to prevent further tumor growth. If there is uncertainty, some 'bridging' procedure might be advisable. This will slow down tumor growth during the waiting time. Chemoembolisation is one such method. There might be benefit in combining this with another treatment modality. We discussed RFA [radiofrequency ablation]. This might be difficult for at least one of the lesions, which is located next to the caval vein: this location makes this method less effective (heat is readily lost due to the blood flow in the vessel) and more dangerous (if heated too much, damage may occur, etc.). Yet another option might be radiotactic radiotherapy (computer-directed towards the lesion).

My hopes would be that screening does not show new problems, that you can be listed on short notice, and that waiting times are short (couple of months at the most).

I wish you, your friends and relatives all the best and good strength in this extremely difficult period. I hope you will be able not to despair but keep on fighting.

If possible, I would be glad to remain informed about your situation.

Sincere regards – Aad van den Berg

I'm extremely thankful to this doctor for taking the trouble to write all this down. I now have a clearer picture and don't have to try to explain to others what is happening.

A whole week of new tests. Some are being repeated. The rumours about getting on the transplant list are becoming stronger. I'm staying at Kyra's place, which is close to the hospital. Little Arabella keeps me entertained and in the right mood to face all this. This morning we went with my youngest son, Marius, my closest family, to the hospital to have a meeting and discuss all the things that can go right and that can go wrong before and after the transplant. I think we're all strong enough to cope with the emotional ups and downs and be patient with one another. As long as I can pass these tests I have a chance. A transplant is not something to look forward to either, but it would give me hope, and hope brings life.

16 June. A hospital bed is like a throne with a view. There's so much splendid detail in the people around me. Some eyes are fearful, others full of hope. Nurses come and go: some are interested in their patients, other do their job and move on. Nursing is still a special profession. More rewarding in the long run than working in an office. From my window I can see some mountains in the far distance and a large slice of the city in front. It's a clear, crisp, wintry day. Hospitals are huge recycling factories of blood, sweat and ... tears.

A friendly lady has come to see me. She has to evaluate whether I'm emotionally strong enough to face a transplant. We talk and connect. I need to talk. Have been too silent. I talk too much but she understands. She believes in God and in prayer and in a way I envy her, but we're both human beings – we care and feel comfortable in one another's company.

This morning the whole physical procedure of transplant was explained: the pros, the cons – the frustrations – the hopes and sacrifices. When you see the photographs of diseased livers and all the intricate technical details about the operation you realise that this is a big task – that the road ahead is difficult and will involve a lot of dedicated people. Life will never be the same, but at least now I have a slight opening to another chapter – a new horizon might be opening up. Very different from what I had before, but maybe with more poignancy, more care and creativity.

Today I find nothing but kindness and love from the people who are looking after me. New blood is being taken, more scans, more trips to the various departments and talking to various doctors. Everything I encounter and go through, I've seen in various films or documentaries. Even when it interested me, the full impact never registered. I was always too busy. Cancer happens to other people.

But now, a little flutter of hope has come my way. For the first time in those six months of confusion and despair, grief and anxiety. I feel a little more optimistic about my physical condition. Soon I will know if a transplant is at all possible.

The sacred ancient text the *Bhagavad-Gita* says that love is interwoven with light, love leads to light, but this light is not ours. It's given to us by the divine grace of the universe. What matters is not to think much, but to love much, because all creation comes from love and if we want to live more we have to love more. I have cancer. I was told, 'You have so many weeks, months to live.' I'm still here because I probably started to love more. My friends and the people who really care have helped me to see this love. Now I can give more. Whereas at first, I thought I had nothing to give. There's a soft evening glow caressing the window. I want to say to the world – I have enough love for all of you … I've moved away from my existence into another, rather distant world. The truth and reality I find there is not as gruesome as the truth and reality I have lived with for the last six months.

I am home for the weekend. What a luxury. I rearrange my room a little, clean up and sit in the sun. There is nothing I want to take from anyone or anywhere, and nothing to give. Living on the edge of the void has advantages. You feel more in tune with life, less confused. You realise how unique and very beautiful life is. 'It's the people, oh the people,' says Sheila Florence in *A Woman's Tale*. If it weren't for the people, it would even be possible to believe in God!

One wonders at times what possesses the human race to behave so badly on this planet. They call you naive when you're not greedy and stupid, when you believe in peace. The history of Man is the history of madness. We've suffered more at the hands of each other than through natural disasters. We have slaughtered, by our own hands, millions of our own species because of greed and blindness. We seek death and destruction as much as life and happiness. Our civilisation has betrayed our true potential *and* our spirit. God didn't create us. We created Him/Her. It's so easy to explore and exploit the metaphysical needs of the individual. The whole concept of God doesn't come from God, but from professional believers. Most wars are being fought in the name of their God. What a miserable and mean excuse. 'God is the manifestation of power in Nature,' said Jesuit priest Paul Tillich, in his *The Shaking of the Foundation*, and I agree.

Today I receive an email from Werner Herzog. He writes about the forest and the birds and the view into the distance and how he hopes that this might give me a moment of cheer in the joyless ward of the hospital. Werner says that I should keep writing and working on my next screenplay and ultimately go under while shooting the film, or the next, or the next after that.

He's right. Werner himself has overcome many obstacles. The legendary story of the making of *Fitzcarraldo* is well known. A friend brought Werner to my place some thirty-five years ago. 'I am Werner Herzog' he said. I thought he was an impostor or someone who carried the same name. He was wearing a white hat like a twentieth-century explorer. It was only later during our conversation that I suddenly realised that this was the real Werner Herzog! Throughout the years we've kept contact and meet up in strange places. He acted in my film *Man of Flowers* and I photographed and played a small part in his film *Where the Green Ants Dream*. He's still as prolific as ever and is one of the few personal filmmakers who use the cinema as a means of self-expression and who has retained his independence and integrity.

❧

Three days of selective eating then fasting. Weak and nauseous, I go into the hospital for a colonoscopy and a gastroscopy. Takes me some time to be able to pronounce these words and find out what happens. I arrive at the hospital feeling pretty sick and tired. My good friend Tony takes me there at six in the morning.

Once again, in no time I'm reduced to a helpless patient in my apron, paper underpants and shoes, and a plastic cover for my head. A large man in a wheelchair is being pushed along by a small woman wearing a tightly knitted wig. It looks like a helmet. From a distance I think it is a hat. We laugh hysterically and hide our faces. We go upstairs and I book in as usual. Same questions – different people, but they are kind, and one elderly nurse even knows one of my films and the actors who played in it. Then the waiting game begins again, interrupted by various nurses and doctors asking questions. Although I couldn't sleep last night, I'm not tired, slightly anxious, halfway through reading *The Setting Sun*, a stunning Japanese novel by Osamu Dazai. Like Yukio Mishima, he also committed suicide, and his book explains why. Despair, loneliness, fear of failure, hopelessness of the thinking, feeling, struggling mind. 'When I pretended I couldn't write a novel, people said I couldn't write. When I acted like a liar, people called me a liar. When I acted like a rich man, they started a rumour that I was rich. But when I inadvertently groaned because I was really in pain, they started a rumour that I was faking suffering.'

They've come to take me into the operating room … morphine, oxygen, tubes everywhere. I fall asleep and dream of beasts. A few hours later a nurse wakes me. 'It's all finished. We'll observe you for a while and then send you back to the ward.' My dreams are of the past, of my parents, sisters and brother. We're all so young and walk through long waving fields of longing. Then my children appear, and the tender face and smile of my grandchild.

On the threshold of sleep or awakening, I feel unbearable tenderness and love. My mother rises like a meteor from my singing blood. Oh, dear Mother, dear Mother of my life. I owe you my life, but more importantly, my humanity. How she would suffer now if she were alive and knew the seriousness of my illness. How she would worry and care. 'If anything happens to one of my children, I would not survive,' she once told us. Suddenly tears, rivers of tears. I can't stop. A kind nurse holds my hand, touches my forehead. Meanwhile, talks casually with a patient across the room. From her touch I realise that she cares, that she understands. She gives me great comfort. When I want to thank her, she tells me to be quiet. All these emotions, mixed with memories and dreams, take up only a small part of our lives. Yet that is the essence of life. That is life! The rest is 'cups of tea and talks of you and me', as TS Eliot puts it so aptly.

This week we're waiting for the final verdict. I will know soon if – in spite of my age, lungs and whatever else – I am eligible for a liver transplant.

Michael Jackson dies, and so does the grand master of India strings, Ali Akbar Khan. He died a few weeks ago but I didn't know, although I watch the news daily and read the papers. It wasn't widely reported that – according to Yehudi Menuhin, the greatest musician who ever lived had departed.

The hysteria about Michael Jackson's death is appalling. The world celebrated him then destroyed him. Elvis Presley and many others suffered the same fate. Who can cope with so much meaningless adulation? Personally I'd rather listen to any street singer in India than our castrato, unmelodious, wildly amplified Western performers. Now we have three days of newspaper hysteria and in the midst of all this, I found a small obituary for Ali Akbar Khan.

The sarod is one of the most difficult instruments. It takes many years of training and practice before one can even be called a sarod player. The painter Asher Bilu is the only Western person I know who plays the sarod well. Ali Akbar Khan said that if you practice the sarod for ten years, you may begin to please yourself. After twenty years, you may become a performer and please the audience. After thirty years, you may even please your guru. But you must practise for many more years before you finally become a true artist – then you may please even God. I feel sorry for Michael Jackson: well meaning, naive and probably very gifted, but the adoration of his public destroyed him before he could really blossom.

Three more days before the final assessment in the hospital. I go to the airport to pick up John Hurt and his wife Anwen. John is such a fine and rare human being. We have a wonderful evening. My son Marius has seen more films with John playing a part than I have, and is most impressed. The next day they fly back to England. Will I ever see them again?

So many years ago, John gave his heart and soul to my film *Vincent – the Life and Death of Vincent van Gogh*. We spent three days in a small studio in London recording John's voice as the voice of Vincent. Three crucial days that have kept this film alive as if we made it yesterday. The only words in the film that were not written by Vincent in his letters to his brother Theo are 'I wish I knew it.' Overcome by frustrations and emotions, these are the very last words John whispers to himself. They came from his heart and thus were left in the film. They sound true and real. Throughout the years we meet occasionally or exchange emails. Vincent van Gogh somehow sealed a friendship that we've never questioned.

❧

Then our visit to the hospital. 'You must bring your family, otherwise the surgeon will not see you.' We walk into a deserted waiting room. We are nervous but don't want to show it. Kyra and Marius sit away from me, looking through women's magazines. I'm hiding behind my newspaper, and walk to the counter now and then to see if there's anyone at all hiding in the labyrinth of corridors. Kyra begs me to sit down. Finally one of the coordinators of the test program comes to collect a few chairs, then ushers us into a small office to meet the surgeon. Some wild thoughts go through my mind. 'A transplant is the only thing that can save me. I'm too old for a transplant! My lungs must be riddled with cancer; my heart must be weak and probably diseased.' But I also think, 'Why didn't they stop the endless testing and the scanning if there is no point in continuing?' The surgeon starts to talk. I look at his sympathetic face, then at my dear children. I miss Ezra, my eldest son, who's working in Bangkok and couldn't be with us.

It slowly dawns on me that the surgeon is telling us that I'm on the transplant list. I've been activated! I've been given a flutter of hope. A light has appeared above the mountains in the distance. For almost six months there was no hope, no hope at all. We depart with deep gratitude, with endless tears that are bursting to get out. We sit in the cafe downstairs, smiling, laughing, crying – eating fatty cakes and holding hands.

A few days later, Kyra, Arabella and I attend a meeting of the pre-transplant education support group. It's a special meeting for children of patients on the transplant waiting list, with the family of a liver recipient. There're also various nurses, dieticians and coordinators introducing themselves. The recipient family is gently asked to talk about their reaction and how they coped. The father, who went through the operation, jokes that it was easy for him because he was asleep and generally felt so sick and drugged that the emotional impact only hit him in retrospect. The mother and the oldest daughter, probably about sixteen, emphasise the strain on the family and what they did to cope.

I think the youngest girl is thirteen or fourteen, rather big for her age. She is asked how she managed. There's silence. The girl hides her face in her mother's bosom, and then looks at the circle surrounding her. She looks at each one of us. Then, out of the very depth of her being, a primal scream echoes through the room. It cuts through our hearts, pierces our bones. She screams once more, bewildered by her own sound. The mother weeps with her, and Kyra, who is standing behind me, holds me so tight that it hurts. Nobody speaks for a while. Almost everyone is too overcome. I think we all feel her agony and pain and how much she suffered through her father's difficult journey. It was all contained in her howl, which found its roots through time and space – embracing many centuries and then caught and trapped her like a caged animal.

Now life has changed a fair bit. I am fully aware of the many pitfalls and problems facing us, but that little flutter of hope has changed something deep inside. Maybe I'm going to live after all. I'm ready for it.

❧

I sleep badly in the next few days. Don't know why. I now have time to go and see old friends whom I haven't seen for years or occasionally met in passing. It's a whole new experience after years of concentration on my work and the children. Now I don't have to rush back to the editing room, or research something related to the film I'm making. I will always have the time now for everything. Every day given to me is a bonus. We all live on borrowed time. There is no other time.

❧

'I think that Cox saw Nijinsky, not as a madman, but as a man too inspired to be sane,' says Roger Ebert in an appreciation he wrote as an introduction to a small retrospective of my films in Melbourne. It's a brilliant way of describing the agony and the ecstasy of a true artist. Only another true artist could put it this way. And Roger, known as a film critic, is a great artist. After some horrendous cancer operations he lost his voice, the ability to use his neck, and needs to be fed through a tube in his stomach. A blow that would kill an ordinary man cannot kill the artist. Roger now writes with more insight, vision, poetry and wit, and raises his pen with fury against any exploitation in the film world. A lesser artist would've surrendered to the cancerous demons that invaded his body. Roger survived all that because he has something to say, something to give. When he heard that I had joined the cancer ward, he and his wife, Chaz, gave me enormous comfort and warmth with the exchange of emails and favourite DVDs. He offered me a lifeline.

❧

This morning, another scan of lungs and liver. Don't want these scans any more. Can't be good for the body, and I'm a little afraid that they might find something else that could put my transplant on hold or they might have to cancel it. Still functioning reasonably well. Get tired and don't sleep. Wake up with headaches and a dizziness that comes and goes during the day. Have always refused to let anyone look after me. Now I want to be looked after, but there isn't really anyone there. That is not really true – they're plenty of good and fine people who would go out of their way to look after me, but I'm probably not ready yet to call upon them. My dear friend from London would sacrifice everything to help and keep me. I know her love for me and feel it, but she's so much younger and has a young child who needs her. Also she lives on the other side of the world and has her own career and family to cope with.

☙❧

This morning I dream that a new liver, heart and lungs had been put into me while I was sleeping. 'Why not tell me?' I ask. 'Besides, I only need a new liver.' The nurse tells me they didn't tell me because I haven't washed my hands. Then I notice that on the bed poles, taps have been fitted with hot and cold water. They want me to wash my hands right through the day because future transplants would have to be done by me as they didn't have enough surgeons and staff to look after everyone. 'But I've got a new liver – don't need another one, and the other organs you've transplanted I'd like to give back to you!' 'Wish it were that simple,' says the nurse. She starts to put gaffer tape on my chest and stomach. 'We've got this from your office,' says the nurse. I protest. Gaffer tape, which is used often in film production, is pretty vicious stuff and very hard to remove. I used it once on a slate roof and the roof didn't leak for over ten years. In fact, I fixed the roof with this very tape. 'But why didn't you use normal tape – the tape you use here for after an operation?' 'You're a filmmaker and we've found that these people are difficult to keep together. The stronger the tape, the better it is for you.' Meanwhile I start to pull some of the tape away from my stomach. It hurts like mad – hair and skin comes off – then the stomach opens and small organs, like little planets, have attached themselves to the tape. The nurse screams, forces the tape back and puts another layer of thick black tape on top. I'm now completely tied down to the bed with gaffer tape.

ৰ০ৰ

Another night of no sleep. My pulse suddenly goes up and I have difficulty breathing. So very tired, yet no sleep comes my way. Even though I have been thrown a lifeline, I'm now more uncertain, vulnerable and physically weak. I was doing so well and felt strong. I remember the young girl who howled when asked how her father's transplant had affected her. I can still feel her pain. It settled somehow in my bones and in my heart. I could've been gone by now, but I'm still alive. I wanted to live and here I am – coping and loving and even making plans. Why then am I disturbed and my body refuses to lie down and rest? Is something else brewing inside or going to happen? No, nothing can happen. I will not give way to negative thought. I must be stronger than that. I must inspire life within me, and around me.

ৰ০ৰ

Today I'm going back to the hospital for more blood tests and to talk to the surgeon. He tells me that I'm doing well – that the chemo worked and the cancer has retreated for a while. From a doomed species with no future at all, I've almost become complete enough to join the human race again. Now I have some space and time to wait for a liver donor. Australia has the lowest rate of organ donation in the Western world.

It seems to come from a lack of public education, different cultural attitudes to the disposal of bodies, superstition, and a reluctance to address the prospect that one day we will all die. In Australia, organ donation works on an 'opt in' system, whereby everyone who has not given consent is not a donor. People here die or get too weak before a new liver is found. The same with other organs. Spain, on the other hand, has the highest rate. Their system is 'opt out', or 'presumed consent', by which everyone who has not refused is a donor.

In my view, too many disagreements occur because of various religious convictions. I don't understand what difference it makes whether one is buried or burned, with the liver, heart, lungs in place or without them. I wonder what happens if a Seventh Day Adventist minister, a rabbi, imam, Catholic priest or strict Protestant vicar needs a transplant or one of their children can only be saved through a transplant. Would they decide to let their child die rather than try to save them through a transplant?

Now, for almost a full month, I've lived the life of a potential recipient. Quite a surreal experience. Although it can take years before a donor is found – you have to be available twenty-four hours a day. Every time the phone rings, the heart jumps and one wonders. Now I'm getting used to it and pick up the phone without thinking about the hospital. Ezra, my son from the East, arrives from Bangkok. When Marius returns from his short holiday in Brisbane, I'll have my three children together. This is only the fourth time for this to happen. I'm proud of them. They're fine, upstanding human beings who have survived a most unorthodox upbringing remarkably well.

❧❦

The days are crisp and sunny, with much blue in the sky. I walk down to the bay and stare across the waters. Cargo boats wait in line to get into port. The bay is quite rough. In spite of the bright sun, there's a cold wind blowing in from the east and patches of rain splash down unexpectedly.

The true process in Man is the progression of an inner vision. That's what Vincent van Gogh meant when he said, 'Isn't life given to us to become richer in spirit?' My children are happy to see one another. Although they all have different mothers, they're similar and even look like sister and brothers. It gives me great joy to see them together.

❧❦

My little empire appears to be crumbling. At first, Kyra and I try to chase the money owed to us. It could save my life. People who owed me money are supportive, but not one, not even in the face of my death, will return one dollar. I won't elaborate. It's too appalling. I realise that my reserves need to be built up because no money can be generated for a long time. Arts curator Maudie Palmer, who's one of the first friends I made when I returned here in 1965, encourages me to explore and exploit my humble beginnings as a stills photographer, and after thirty years of not having touched a still camera, I take a series of photographs of dancer Delia Silvan with the camera and tripod that had been hidden all that time.

Delia is a delicate flower of great beauty and integrity, and in a few days we produce a series of photographs called *Evening*

Light. We found a simple, singular way of expression – beauty enclosed in the prison of light. It started as a financial exercise, but of course lost its way in that vast landscape of possibilities. Some of these photographs may be a little too disciplined, but the light burns in each one with longing and defiance. In my threatened existence the light should be fragile, tinted through dust, heavy skies. That's what I thought would happen, but this light is strong and bright and suggests hidden colours. One is never really in charge of the inner gods or demons. It's only by making something that its purpose manifests itself and, if one is in tune, offers a direction to take. A film too, in my not so humble opinion, is always made in the making. As soon as it gathers a life of its own, one knows one is on the right pathway and all one has to do is keep up with its force and have faith. Life itself is mostly a matter of fate and not of choice. People tend to believe that they're somehow in charge. Thank the good Lord, Krishna, Allah, Buddha and all other Gods that we're not.

ॐ

Gallery owner Charles Nodrum offers exhibition space in his inner-city gallery. We decide to add some early black-and-white photographs in another room for balance. The show does reasonably well, but the main thing is that it receives interest in other un-exhibited material. My early career as a photographer blossoms once again, and brings some much needed financial rewards.

At the opening, a woman stops me several times. 'I am Suzi'. I find it hard to concentrate and talk to anyone at length, and try to ignore her. But she is persistent, takes me to the room with the old black-and-white photographs and says, 'I'm the model in number twenty-four.' A volcano spews fire. Here is the missing link I'd been looking for in the puzzle of the past. I hadn't recognised her at all, but suddenly I remember her immense beauty and the sweetness of her smile. In the few encounters we'd shared in the far distant past, I'd experienced an extraordinary sexual awakening through her. Body of my body, flesh of my flesh. Ecstasy stored away for centuries made inner and outer become one and melted into one softly boiling river. I'd never met an uninhibited soul like that. She was beautiful and glowing with womanhood. It shook my foundations. Through her, the artist in me thrived and I learned how to merge the inner and outer and celebrate the outer with the same degree of mysticism and human touch as the inner. I'd totally forgotten how crucial she was to my development. Some forty years later, Grandpa Me and Grandmother Suzi have become friends again.

಄ೋ಄

It's almost five in the morning. Sleep comes and goes. A dream of some confusion throws me out of bed. In the dream, I try to answer my phone but I have to get out of bed as it is positioned out of reach. My skin is dripping with sweat as I answer a call from the hospital. 'You ordered a transplant,' a female voice says. 'Yes, a liver transplant!' 'We don't have livers – we have sausages and cut meat.' A familiar figure approaches. For a split second I know who it is, but then I lose it. I think it's the butcher who supplies meat to the hospital. I suspect him of terrible crimes. A small woman who comes with him starts to throw eggs against the wall. I get into a wild panic – maybe they have my new liver waiting for me at the hospital and these people are trying to steal it from me. I sneak out of the back door and start running, but then realise I don't know which direction the hospital is. The phone rings again, but remains out of reach.

I indeed wake up in a pool of sweat. The hospital did ring this morning to ask whether I'd had a certain blood test last week. There was no record of it. The call gave me a bit of a shock, which must've stayed in my consciousness until the dream released it.

It's now a waiting game. Nobody knows how long it will take to find a new liver. Sometimes I despair and feel trapped, but then have to tell myself how very lucky I am. Apart from the nausea, the headaches and the sleepless nights, I am alive, and have a true solid chance to bounce back to life. This was never expected when it all started.

⊷⊷

It's such a blessing to be surrounded by my three children. Ezra can't stay too long, but our connection is growing stronger, as is our friendship and trust. They are fine generous people – loving, humorous and humane.

It's early morning. A bright new day with a clear blue sky and sunlight flooding the kitchen. There's a review of *Salvation* on the table. The film came and went. I'd almost forgotten we ever made it. If you don't have a large advertising budget, no film can succeed in this country. The review has a funny headline, 'Thank the good Lord for eccentric artists.' I rarely read reviews, but the headline made me smile. I like the light-hearted approach, unpretentious and revealing. Don't see myself as an eccentric, though I must admit a certain fascination with eccentric characters. However, when people refer to me as an eccentric, I always look around to find out to whom they're referring.

Every morning, two large magpies pay me a visit. They tap on the kitchen window and sing a duet until I come out and feed them some cheese or meat for breakfast. One has grown very cheeky; she sits on my shoulder and offers her primeval call right next to my ear. I go downstairs and check the endless emails that have come flooding in since my illness.

๛

Kyra arrives and, together with Marius, we hop in the car and go to the hospital. As they're taking blood we keep joking, and when I'm dressed in one of those humiliating hospital gowns they say goodbye. I'm now on my own with their kisses on my cheeks and their warmth and love in my heart. I'm so lucky. My children are wonderful human beings.

When I return from the scanning and the prodding, I'm so tired that I fall asleep and another dream enters my consciousness. We're in a courtyard of a red building. The bricks are like large sandstones and should be yellow. A group of Swedish workers are discussing a Swedish film. Roger Ebert doesn't agree with the general opinion. Does Roger speak Swedish? I ask him. He says, 'They're not speaking Swedish, they're discussing a Swedish film.' Roger is speaking, what a surprise. I'm so pleased that he can speak again even though he doesn't get his facts right. He senses my thoughts and says, 'Best to ignore me speaking, nobody has noticed anyway.'

√

There is a two-day conference on my films at Melbourne University and straight after that, the opening of the photographic exhibition. So many people from the past – so many good friends – appear. It is all very touching, but also extremely exhausting. It's common knowledge that I am 'riddled with cancer'; bad news travels at the speed of light. Not many people know that there is a flutter of hope, that I am not totally doomed, that I might actually outlive them all. Find myself talking to people without having the slightest idea who they are … not a nice thing to admit, but true. There is always some familiar touch – something that stirs old memories – but they don't find fertile ground, I've gone blank. I'm sure the chemo that's still lurking in my body and mind has something to do with an almost total lack of memory.

August. Late at night. Silence in the streets and in my heart. My brother-in-law sent me a quote by French philosopher Ernest Renan – 'Man is not placed on the earth merely to be happy, nor is he placed merely to be honest, he's here to accomplish great things through society. To arrive at nobleness and to outgrow the vulgarity in which the existence of almost all individuals drags on.' Not so sure about the last bit … The phone rings. I'm already in bed reading.

'Tracey from the Austin Hospital. We have a liver that might suit you. There's two possible recipients, but it looks promising for you.' I can't breathe for a while. I realise I have nothing ready to take with me, jump out of bed and quickly pack a toothbrush, a shaver and a change of clothing. Check my email but the line is dead. Ring Kyra. Don't want to really wake her, but she would expect it. I drive off, forget my mobile phone, return home and then proceed towards Kyra's home. On the way, a million and one thoughts cross my mind. Memories of a distant past, planes in the sky and war raging all around, my mother's soft embrace, the first day at school. Then the practical need of staying on the road becomes essential. Almost lose my way along a very familiar route. Kyra is waiting for me, looking a little pale and tired. Off we go to the hospital Emergency Department. Straight away, blood pressure and pulse is taken, and after an X-ray we go upstairs, where I finally land in a single room and much blood is taken and carried off.

Now I'm left alone and think of all the things I've forgotten to do. People walk in and out of my room. I feel very social and want to talk, but everyone is too busy.

Ulli Beier and his wife Georgina are coming the day after tomorrow. We met in New Guinea so many years ago. That same night, Anoja Weerasinghe arrives from Sri Lanka. She was one of the three actresses in my film *Island* and is now a fine and noble crusader for her people and her country. What will they do when I'm not there? This is probably the last time I can pass on some information as I expect to be out of it for quite a few days. Maybe I shouldn't worry about anything, but that's not my nature.

Kyra has gone home for a while. She needs to sleep. Even though I took a sleeping pill before I went to bed, I'm not tired. I feel remarkably calm. This is a big moment in my life. Still don't understand why all this had to happen to me. Only twenty years ago, before a liver transplant was possible, I would've died. Now I sit here in a single room with a large sign on the wall 'NIL ORALLY'. Waiting for the doctors to inspect the liver they have and decide who's going to be the recipient. Meanwhile, I have to be ready and standing by.

The door of my room is open. A man is screaming in the corridor. I don't know what language. People rush towards him, calm him down, drug him, put him out of his misery. A scream wells up inside my heart – a silent scream. My life no longer belongs to me.

ॐॐ

It's now early morning. I have a little sleep with no dreams.

A female doctor comes to take notes and admit me to the hospital officially. She is called away without finishing the job. I still don't know if the liver they have will be mine. The doctor and the nurse who have been attending to me wish me well with the operation. The nurse claims that I will be on my feet within a few days. Will the operation go ahead? Everything seems all right and in place, but there's another person whose need for a new liver might be more urgent than mine.

Nijinsky wrote in his diary, 'I feel a piercing stare from behind, I feel that people want to harm me, but I will not fight and my enemy will be disarmed. They may wound me, but they cannot kill me. I know how to suffer.' The people here want to help me, save me, but the 'piercing stare from behind' is a metaphor I've been living with for many years. To me it means that we're being watched, being talked about; negative energy is being put out there that needs to be counterbalanced. The 'piercing stare' now is probably the small chance that I might not wake up from the operation, that death is lurking nearby and that I will have to fight. When things were really bad and there wasn't any hope of survival, I stopped listening to music. It made me too sad. Now I would love to have Mozart playing in my room, or an Italian opera, the gypsy music from the Balkans or the sarod of Ali Akbar Khan.

I think that music is the basis of all creation. At the first 'rough cut' screening of *Father Damien* in Brussels, Theo van Gogh and Paul Grabowsky, the composer, are sitting next to me. There's a moment when the music soars and merges perfectly and completely with the moving image, a magic moment of bliss. We share something higher, beyond earthly matters. Paul's face glows in the dark. We both know we've hit that 'high note'. Theo brings us right back to earth when he whispers, 'Yes, yes alright … But the producers won't get it'. Theo was right. The producers didn't recognise 'the hand of God' and later destroyed the glory of the film. Don't know why I'm thinking about this now, something to do with the longing for good music.

A young Chinese doctor comes to ask a few questions, once again examines the abdomen and then needs my signature on a form just in case something goes wrong with the operation. Nothing will go wrong.

From where I sit, I can look into a long corridor with all sorts of people starting their daily duties. Nurses appearing and disappearing. A cleaning lady makes her way towards me. We immediately become engaged in a lively discussion. So many people have been killed in her country – so much suffering she's seen and experienced. She asks me why fish smell from the head and not from the rear! I don't know the answer. Apparently it's because the people at the head of her country are smelly fish – of course they also smell from the rear, but it doesn't compare with the vile smell that comes from their heads. She fled with her husband – likes the safety of Australia, even though she can only get a job as a cleaner – but is very homesick. Every time she has earned enough money, she goes 'home' to regenerate and feel complete again. When she talks about the beauty of her town and the surrounding forests, her eyes grow moist. Another cleaner enters, and complains about her slow performance. She silently continues and disappears into the corridor. The other cleaner wipes some imaginary dust off a ridge and shakes her head.

It's eight-thirty in the morning. I'm waiting to be called

either to the operating theatre or to be sent home. Kyra rings, and can't understand that I still haven't heard. We just have to be patient and ready to accept whatever happens. It's an extraordinary thought – in a few hours I could be facing a huge operation that will have large repercussions for the rest of my life. Now it's ten-thirty, and I still don't know. If I've learnt anything in the last few months, it's patience and the acceptance of a life of uncertainty.

Thinking about the person who has left this Earth. Organ donation is a phenomenal advancement in science. Part of a dead person is going to live within me. I must honour this soul and the people who loved him or her by doing something beautiful with the rest of my life. Of course nothing has happened yet, but that's the plan.

A doctor has just come in, together with the psychiatrist I spoke to earlier. 'This is a dummy run. The liver has gone to a needy child.' That I'm even being considered and already high on the list has given me such a boost in confidence that I instantly feel resigned to this news. Pity, but I will get my liver. I have to be patient and strong. Kyra has more difficulty coping with this news. They let us wait until a nurse and a psychiatrist are available to help us cope. Very considerate, but we're coping very well and should've been home and asleep by now.

I'm beyond the disappointment now. Still complete – my body isn't scarred from head to toe. Ulli Beier and his wife, Georgina, are still staying at my home. So is Anoja Weerasinghe, my Sri Lankan actress friend. Ulli and Georgina lived in Africa, ran workshops and published many books on Africa and its people. Then they went to New Guinea to teach at the new university of Port Moresby. Ulli is tired and feels old, but when animated, his old spark and sense of humour returns. They retired and went to live in Australia, but we've all concluded that this was a mistake. They aren't good at living in the West. It's as simple as that.

Anoja was a big star in her own country and in the East. I travelled once with her and her husband through Sri Lanka and witnessed close up how she was adored and loved by her people, including the prime minister at the time. While crossing the street, he said to me, 'You're my bodyguard. They will never attack me when I'm with a foreigner.' A few weeks later he was blown up, together with some forty people of his government.

During the 2000 presidential election, Anoja got involved in politics and decided to back the opposition leader. Her popularity was a great asset. She addressed seven rallies, gave emotional speeches that were very much appreciated by the ordinary, struggling people, but her whole political career lasted some three days. After the old president was reinstated, Anoja's house was burned down and thugs from the Government waited with machetes and guns for her to emerge from the burning ruins, to rape and then kill her. They'd forgotten to check whether she was home. It was a deciding step for Anoja to change her life and her future.

Now Anoja is a Buddhist nun. Her long black hair is gone, and instead of gracing the silver screen with her exotic beauty, she's looking after tsunami victims and war orphans, which has made her much happier than when she was a popular star.

৵৽

I'm too sick now to function on a daily level. The nausea and headaches used to come and go, but now the nausea has settled and the lack of energy forces me to stay in bed.

In this morning's newspaper I see two small articles that draw my attention. The northern part of Sri Lanka is heavily flooded. Some 200,000 people are homeless. After the war and the tsunami in which so many perished, nature turns against them again. A second article concerns a patch of land in Los Angeles, next to the grave of Marilyn Monroe. This patch of soil is becoming available because the widow of the man who's been laid to rest here has decided to have his bones removed and put the patch up for auction. She has been struggling with a million-dollar mortgage and expects to get a million or so for the land, poor woman! Already some ardent Marilyn lovers have come forward. They are keen to contemplate an underground affair with Marilyn. This is reported in all seriousness, by a serious newspaper. A week later, I hear that the land next to Marilyn's went for $4 million at auction, four times more than what was expected!

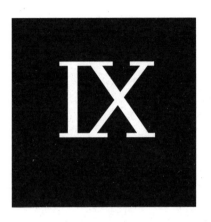

September. Went to the hospital for various blood tests and to talk to the doctor. My transplant is still on the cards but nobody knows how long it will take. I'm high on the list, but my blood group is quite rare and livers are also quite rare and hard to come by. I have to wait and be patient, but soon I will be too old for a transplant. Once the mind keeps tossing the same thought or idea around, the 'obsession of thought' rubs off on all and everything around – especially my dreams.

It's dark in a long corridor leading towards a sunlit garden. I don't understand why the outside light doesn't creep into the corridor. A trolley arrives loaded with pieces of fresh meat. Two people wearing masks are pushing the trolley. As they get closer I realise that the trolley is loaded with livers. Small ones, big ones, old and new. One liver falls off and splashes onto the floor. A man in black picks up the liver and beckons me to come forward. The ceiling above opens with thousands of flickering stars. Now I'm on the trolley with a masked person right above me. A voice proclaims, 'Your transplant must be done at short notice in order to prevent further tumour growth.' I realise that three or more livers have been put inside me. I scream out, 'Too much, too much!' No one takes any notice. I'm asked to paint a picture of a hand on my stomach. Then a hand comes out of my stomach and starts to fight with the hand I've painted. The man in black tells me that if I admit to having two livers they will let me go. I'm happy with two livers. The man says, 'We're experimenting with the liver shortage: with two livers you can procreate and we can harvest a small liver every few months. You're helping us greatly.' Then I walk into a large field of green – long grass that waves in the wind like in Tarkovsky's *Mirror*. The green sticks to my skin like oil paint.

☙❧

It's now a week or two later. Maybe three weeks. Time 'becomes unreal in solitude'. There isn't much to report, apart from my daily routine, which is very similar to the time before I became ill. I find that the day hardly registers; the night lasts longer, because I don't sleep much. I can't. Waiting for the hospital to ring has become a futile obsession. Some psychic powers seem to have come my way. Maybe this is the way we used to communicate. I only have to think of a person and they will ring or email me. It happens almost every day – mainly with women friends or very close male friends.

Today they're photographing the back of my eyes. There is a disease called Age-related Muscular Degeneration or AMD. AMD is the most common cause of visual impairment in individuals over fifty. Although I'm almost seventy, I don't regard myself as that old. It's silly to give people a number.

Georgina Beier left a DVD behind: Mitsuko Uchida playing Mozart. Maybe this waiting game makes me hypersensitive, but it moved me from the very beginning to the very end. An immensely beautiful performance by this powerful yet fragile pianist. When she doesn't touch the piano, she conducts with overwhelming love for the music. She gives, then gives some more, then gives all. As long as we have people creating, producing such beauty, such tenderness, such deeply felt emotions, there's hope in the world – there's a future. I'm very grateful and wish I could share this with people I know or don't know.

Although it gets a little cold at night, there's a touch of spring in the air. The pear tree in front of my window already carries a bit of white blossom. There're no leaves yet to be seen. The blossom of the pear tree is one of my most intimate childhood memories. There was a pear tree in the open garden next door, and every spring the petals would cross the rusty wire fence and dance down on our side like silent snowflakes. Makes me yearn to be in Europe and walk the fields outside my hometown. Makes me yearn for my lost old European roots. We used to run after the dancing petals trying to catch them. When we caught one, they seemed to just disintegrate, evaporating in the palms of our hands.

❧❧

The phone rings in my dreams. It's the hospital informing me that they've found a suitable donor. Is it finally all happening? I lie back for a moment, ready to start packing, to ring Kyra and make arrangements. Unfortunately, I fall asleep again and don't wake until early morning. I wake up in a panic. 'Oh my God, I'm at least five hours behind! They must be very anxious at the hospital! I can't find their number. This is what I've been waiting for so long!' Then it occurs to me that maybe the call was part of the dream. I remember it was a male voice with a slight accent, which seemed a bit odd. Now I'm confused. Will I ring them and ask whether there was a call? Shall I have breakfast and wait? I'm too embarrassed to ring the hospital. I talk to my daughter, who wisely suggests that they would have called again if it were real. I decide to have breakfast and read the paper. There are no more phone calls.

The intricate workings of the mind or the brain go on even during sleep or dreaming. I'm now three months into this waiting game. Everything has become even more uncertain. But I'm still breathing. I am still living and that certainly wasn't the plan some months ago. But my dreams are disturbing. They all lead toward the obsessive search for a transplant. In my dreams I find metaphors, but then they lose their obscurity. Everything celestial turns to blood, sweat and tears – becomes purely physical. A voice inside me screams out, 'I want to live'.

The Tibetan doctrine says that in eating, sleeping, fearing and copulating, Man and beast are alike. Then it claims that humankind exceeds beast by engaging in religious practices. If this were true I would rather join the animal kingdom. Animals usually do things for good reasons. Much of mankind's action has no purpose, is destructive rather than constructive – without any sense of love and beauty. We receive glimpses of paradisiacal beauty from the primal world of land, sea and sky. Beauty is always shrouded in mystery, for without mystery there's no beauty. Our rapport with nature is a religion to me and much more godly than all man-made religions or worshiping of deities.

సం

These days I get up early, sometimes walk in the dark towards the ocean and sit at the end of the pier waiting for the light to spread across the waters. I become part of the daily birth of the light, part of its power, and part of its struggle to burn through the dark. Then the sea overtakes me and washes away all wounds. My dreams are now thick with memory – country roads in France mix with the faces of children in the East. Fields of flowers bring erotic memories of first lovers. Forests of my youth pulsate with mysterious images of foreign deities and illuminations of past and future. I write:

At the edge of the woods I hear children play.
Their small silhouettes against an evening sky.
Music from within the forest embraces, caresses, nourishes.
One dew drop from the morning shines in the dark.
How come it survived the wind and rays of the sun that
brushed past as the trees moved?

'Life is only some kind of sowing time and the harvest is not here,' said Vincent van Gogh. No, the harvest is not here, but did Vincent really expect a harvest? I don't think he did. For him the journey of life was about becoming richer in spirit, finding more freedom of spirit – something most religions oppose. Too often, religion regards itself as the one and only, and is intolerant of other doctrines. Best to stay away from religion and go for the dreaming – the most powerful religion of them all.

The Roman Catholics say, confess all your sins before death, otherwise you may burn forever and ever. Not a kind God who would let this happen. The only thing we have to know is that after every death, life becomes more precious, and we should treat the living with even greater love and care.

The ancient Greeks understood that religion was an abstract nature worship. They found that religion had its origin in the personification of the powers of nature. Either Man goes to seek the spirits of his ancestor, the spirits of the dead, or he needs to understand the power working behind the stupendous phenomena of nature. Whatever is the case, he tries to transcend the limitations of the senses. WE need to go beyond, and the first glimpse of it all comes through dreams and visions – not through religion. I tried to write about this in my memoir *Reflections*, but didn't fully understand it at the time. Now it's a little clearer to me.

Children don't distinguish between dreaming and their awakened state. The body is dead during sleep, yet the mind goes on with its intricate workings. Do these workings go on after the body has been dissolved forever? Does the soul escape when the flesh dies? If souls don't die, why do we make so much of saying goodbye? When people die in their sleep, do their dreams travel on? When the person whose liver I might receive, dies while he or she is dreaming a beautiful dream, does this dream leave an imprint on the organ – as it finds a new home? We all have deeply rooted metaphysical needs, which make us vulnerable. They also make us human, oh so human.

I have two backgrounds, two early lives as a youth – growing up during and after the Second World War and my early times in Australia – although in my early twenties I was still a child, and knew and understood little of the so-called real world.

I was born three weeks before the war started in Holland – when the Germans invaded our small town on the border with Germany. They fought a major battle in the park in front of the house where I was born. My mother told me many years later that when she took me to the window overlooking the park, she covered my eyes, afraid that some of the horror and brutality would register. Most of my youth in Holland I remember in fine detail, but my first visits to Australia remain quite obscure. A special program had brought me here the first time, to learn about Australia either through study or work and then return to Europe to promote the place. I was shy, sexually repressed and felt inferior to all. I went to Melbourne University and fell helplessly in love. All those months of isolation had created a certain imbalance in my system. I loved her desperately and wanted to marry her. Fortunately she stopped me. After a year I returned to Holland, but came back partly because I was still helplessly in love. When later we sadly separated, I started to free myself from the shadows of the past and find my own pathway. I discovered that soft singing of the blood. I realised that I was a traveller, an outsider, and maybe, an artist.

The close proximity of death makes life more interesting, they say – but that has always been the case. Life is extremely interesting and needs to be lived with all of our hearts and senses. Otherwise we deny all depth and beauty of existence.

For three-and-a-half months now, I've been waiting for a transplant. It hasn't been an easy time, but I'm alive – with faint dreams of a future. It feels like years. It can take up to three years before a suitable liver can be found. The worst thing about this process is that you can't make any plans, can't look ahead, can't travel. Your life is on hold, or rather, the future is on hold.

So I'm rediscovering the joy of watching films. Because I'm doing some assessing of student films, a home theatre is installed in my apartment. I go into a video shop and out of thousands of films, can't find one single new film that I want to watch. So, back to the classics and films that were made with a conscience. Film can affect us so deeply and linger in our consciousness. A gift from the gods to the very time we live in. That shapes our society, especially the world of our children and their dreams. The Old Masters didn't talk about the commercial potential of their film and what particular audience they had in mind. They knew that film would be a link between the known and the unknown and constantly explored its potential, and then travelled beyond. I wonder, where are the Buñuels, the Bergmans and Fellinis? Their films lasted because they treasured the freedom of expression and painted with a brush free from all commercial demands or the forced exposure of all that is cheap, exterior and painless. My present vulnerability makes me more extreme! Of course there's room for 'entertainment' and films that help people forget and relax.

✄

It's a Saturday afternoon. The rain has been falling incessantly. Although we are well into spring, winter seems to have returned with a vengeance. People complain about the weather, as they complain about their health. In fact, the most popular topics of conversation are the weather and health. People are always inspired by the weather and can talk about their ailment with endless authority. Once I answered 'Have a nice day,' with 'I have other plans.' What I thought was a silly joke was not appreciated or understood at all. Judging from the disapproving looks, I'd committed a serious offence!

In the United States, the debate about the proposed changes to the health system has been raging across the country. I've heard it said many times by Republican senators or TV personalities, 'We have the best health system in the world,' when forty per cent of the population has no health insurance. Why is socialism a dirty word in the world of 'Me first, and don't you touch what I've gathered in my life – that's all mine and mine only'? I worked for it and with God's help, spread some around to local charities and to the church. I saw a man being interviewed in his stupendous home who insisted that tax breaks for the rich were saving America – 'Through my tax break, I can send my wife shopping and help her to buy four pairs of boots instead of one pair. Just think of all the people she will keep in their jobs this way.'

The celebration of the dollar also makes people forget that

they might just have other talents – apart from making money – that could be used creatively and help others less fortunate. They forget too that not all people regard money as the priority of their lives. A public rally in the States showed a man with a big sign: 'Obama is a socialist'. May his sins be forgiven!

I once arrived in Los Angeles with a blocked neck. Apart from the excruciating pain, I couldn't move my head, but managed to find a hospital that could maybe help. It was not a very happy experience. Apart from waiting for hours, my credit card was meticulously examined and the huge amount after one night in hospital was triple checked before they sent me on my merry way. The system itself was extremely grim and although some nurses showed compassion and concern, like most nurses do, the system itself didn't really accommodate much humanity. If I'd fallen ill in such a system with no insurance, I could have lost all, including my life. To have a just society, health should be the same for everybody. I have no insurance, but I'm being treated with care, warmth and affection. A liver transplant in the United States without insurance would be difficult. Australia still has a remarkable health system that tries its utmost to cater for all.

I've found an enormous amount of sheer goodness from nurses, surgeons and doctors. Politicians should be asked to work in a hospital from some years before they're allowed to be elected. At least they would be given a chance to mix with some very fine, caring people and be reminded of their potential as human beings before going on to represent them. I've always been wary of hospitals and have avoided them as much as possible, but I've learned to appreciate the kindness and dedication of a committed nursing staff. They are special people with a special job. In moments of great despair and loneliness I had a tough old nurse stroking my forehead while talking to someone else. It was all done so casually that no one realised that she was helping me through a bad patch, that she knew exactly what was going on and wanted to help and support me without making a fuss.

These people don't meet in boardrooms to plan the launch of a new product or get on the waiting list to become Businessperson of the Year. They simply do their jobs and give and then give some more. They are there when reality and dreams merge, when hallucinations invade the soul and when the loneliness of the long hospital night strangles the heart. I've seen them silently removing a dead body and found within the hour a new body in the bed, a new person gasping for breath. Someone was appalled by the efficiency of their morbid task, but I felt nothing but admiration and respect. Yes, the show must go on, but here we didn't have a show – nothing to show off! They stood tall and strong without reward and did their difficult jobs without complaining.

৵৽

Tomorrow, I return to see my doctor, and the day after I will join a session with various staff, doctors and surgeons. I know they will tell me that four months on the waiting list is nothing. For me, at the moment, four months is a lifetime – as is the next day and the one after that.

৵৽

At the meeting in the hospital I speak to a woman who had been on the waiting list for twenty months. She says she has a rare blood group. I am shocked to hear it is the same as mine. But she is feeling reasonably well and is not in a hurry to receive her transplant. I mention it to the doctor, who admits it is terrible that so very few organs are available, but my case is different. Few liver transplant recipients have liver cancer. Apart from genetic disorders, hepatitis B and C are the major instigators.

I speak to the dietician and a fine woman who looks after social and psychological matters, then have more blood tests, while more appointments are made for repeat scans and X-rays. It is a busy and tiring day, and it is only when I see Kyra arriving with Arabella to pick me up that I realise my emotional state. Had almost forgotten that I am seriously ill, that life is still hanging by a thread. When I sit in the car, it takes some time to be able to speak, to move back to the land of the living. Such a blessing to be with my family – to travel together through the galaxies. We shall always linger on that threshold.

∞∞

I have dinner with my doctor friend James and a young woman from Afghanistan. We joke about livers and how you could cut a liver in two and share it. She likes the idea and thinks with her rare blood group she could really be of use. I ask, 'What is your blood group? I have a similar problem.'

She takes out her wallet with her donor's card – the first person I have met in Australia who actually produces a donor's card – and again it was the same blood group as mine. She generously suggests that we go to the hospital and cut her liver in half. I think it would be better for us to go to Afghanistan, where so many people get killed every day for no reason and leave their organs on the road or in the deserts to be eaten by the vultures or to rot away in the sun. How is it possible that the carnage in Iraq or Afghanistan now hardly registers? In the papers it seems more important to comment on Hollywood stars or a gruesome murder somewhere, than focusing on the enormous human misery – basically created by the West, since Alexander the Great – in this ancient, mystical country.

જ⌀ઈ

Another week has gone by. This waiting game is difficult, especially when I feel that I'm slowly travelling backwards. But without treatment, I would now be gone and would have nothing to worry about. I have to admit that it's more difficult Being than Not Being. Deep down I have this insane belief that there's more life to come – that I shall be able to watch my grandchild grow and love, and that I will bounce back in the filmmaking world with my finest contribution so far. Am I losing my mind?

જ⌀ઈ

A friend sends me a book, *Tiger's Eye*, written by Inga Clendinnen who, some years ago, was struck by a rare and incurable liver disease. The book traces the mental and physical impact of her illness, from spectacular hallucinations to simple observations of the people in her hospital ward. It's also a wonderful memoir – a deeply felt self-portrait by a remarkable writer. She was one of the earliest recipients of a transplant in Australia. It saved her life. We talked on the phone. It is good to discuss her transplant and how she has coped then and now.

Drive some 80 km out of town, I need to see the sky – the stars – need to be free. It's quite telling that one can rarely see the sky at night in the cities. Why do we live like that and don't allow the real roof of the world to protect and shelter us? It is wonderful to lie in the grass, to smell the earth – to feel the damp rising and see layer upon layer of stars appearing above my head. So many galaxies. All of them have their own black holes – their own infinity. I read somewhere that when astrophysicists first discovered black holes in the cosmos they found that psychotic patients had long been familiar with black holes and the trauma of nothingness. Female psychotic patients saw the vagina as the externalisation of the dead zone, the black hole on Earth. And the male patients' need for touch was replaced by a wrenching fear of being touched. In our world of insanity, nobody has control. Everything happens – like snow melting under the sun – like rainfall – or the wind blowing in from the west or the east. It happens. Man is born, lives, dies, not as he wants to, but as it happens. The course of fate cannot be changed. In the midst of this, WE keep searching for meaning or direction, while the answers lie deep within and have been with US from the very beginning. Nothing is perfect except organic forms or relative organic matter. Time and space are not two independent concepts. They're interrelated, forming a single continuum of space–time.

Looking at the 'open sky' at night overrides everything,

makes humankind's activities totally absurd. All organic matter within nature, within the body, relates. Although heavily sedated, I see them invading the arteries around my heart. I see riverbeds rising out of nowhere and I see the universe within my own body. When I wake, it is impossible to stop the river of tears, endless, helpless tears.

⇠⇢

I return from my escape into the night, and become part of the city, part of the streets and the cars and the dying lights again, I feel so removed from society that I could depart here and now. It all seems so utterly useless, so absurd to live a life of routine, of steel and iron, of advertisements and screaming music, of empty material goals. At home I look at a picture of my grandchild, listen to an old gypsy song, change a light bulb. It all starts to make sense again. From above comes light and darkness. In the world of people – from above comes order and demands. People obey orders from above and give their lives for people they don't know. Everybody believes that the people they see on TV or in the papers are in charge. Some are happy that way; others are always struggling with nagging doubt, with uncertainties. Is this what life is? Is this the beginning, is this the end? This is where religions come in and spread their authority, disguised as 'salvation'.

To be vulnerable is to live – if you're not, you die while living a lost life. People who live so-called 'active lives' often have an artificial morality. They don't do anything deliberate in the interest of evil. Yet these people kill one another in the interest of good. Because my life is in the balance, I'm now stronger. I can see and feel the importance of planetary influences. 'Walk out of your heart under the wide sky', said Rilke. I'm trying to separate the physical me from the spiritual me, just in case I lose the physical me. At this very moment I'm fully aware of the enormous benefits my illness has given me. I can see and move freely in between the restrictions of this world and the unlimited potential of the cosmos. Meanwhile, I remain vulnerable. Life will always creep in through the cracks.

Yet I'm on death row and the key to my cell has been lost. Nobody can get in and I can't get out. There's a window high on the wall through which I can observe the sky during the day and the universe at night. Who has the key to my cell? Is it me who has swallowed it, to keep the executioner at bay?

Some years ago, I walked through the local market, and heard Joseph Schmidt singing Puccini. The music came from a small stand with eternal Christmas lights and an old woman selling CDs and DVDs. She was wearing a large hat with artificial flowers – Klimt meets Edward Munch. When she gave me the cover, I recognised Joseph Schmidt and I plunged back through space and time – a young boy walking with his mother through the ruins of our town.

We reach the edge of the woods. Everything here has been left the way it always was. There's an old house half-hidden among the trees. Through an open window, a voice echoing across the fields. Joseph Schmidt singing Puccini. My mother holds me tight, stops in front of the house. I look at her face. She silently weeps.

Later she tells me about Joseph Schmidt, a much loved opera and film star in Germany before the war. He thought his popularity would protect him, but one day the Nazis appeared at one of his concerts and arrested him because of his Jewish background. Before they could kill him, he escaped to Switzerland, where he thought he would be safe. But he was put in a detention centre and died of pneumonia.

I take the CD home and play it in my living room. Everything around me moves, then freezes. Even my heart stops beating for a while. Joseph Schmidt does not exist for me for sixty years. Then he returns and brings intimate memories of my mother and a rare voice full of depth and nostalgia. I go back to the woman with the flowery hat at the market to order more copies. I want to give them to all my friends and family. I want all the copies that were ever made. Fill the world with Joseph Schmidt. But there are no more copies.

❧

As I drive back from the country, I notice a patch of green with small yellow flowers against the gravestones of an old cemetery. It looks so fresh, so innocent, so young. Again, I plunge back through time and space and remember when we moved from the outer suburbs in my small hometown to the inner city. My father is to start his own photographic business in one of the first houses that has been built since the war in the centre of the city. We walk to this house, through the devastated railway station; the track has been cleared for the passing trains. There is a patch of green with tiny yellow flowers in between the railway tracks that looks so young, so fresh, so innocent. Everything else is rusted, twisted iron, broken war equipment and an old train that has probably sheltered many people. That night we sleep in the new house, which isn't far from the railway track. All through the night, trains keep moving, and I wonder and worry about that patch of green in between the railway tracks. Would it be gone in the morning because of all the trains passing?

Haven't thought about this for sixty years. Now in this vulnerable stage, this memory is as clear as if it happened only yesterday. I don't understand though why I can't remember whether I checked it the next morning.

I have dreams of hope, or rather they leave hope behind. Always moving towards a central point. The village square – the centre of town, the heart of the matter. When I arrive – when I dream I've arrived – the centre always lies further away. The centre is never the real centre. There's always another central point further away.

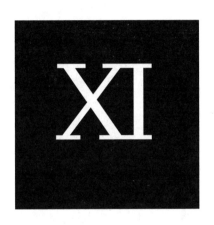

Kyra writes a letter to the surgeon in Holland who's been of such great help in explaining and advising us.

I am Paul Cox's daughter Kyra and wanted to write and ask you a few questions, which I hope you don't mind. If you haven't the time to reply at the moment, I completely understand. I wanted to know a bit more about the transplant/donor process in Holland and if it would be possible for my father to continue there. I feel it would be better for him, professionally and emotionally to be in Europe. He has been approved for transplant here and has of course had all the appropriate tests done. Would he have to go through this testing process again in Holland, or could he take across the existing information and results? He is at the top of the waiting list here and I assume if he were to return to Holland he would be at the bottom of the list again? Would this be different because of the cause of his liver damage? We are unsure if he would have a better chance of earlier transplant here or there due to the different donor culture in Europe. Any information you could give us would be much appreciated. Thank you very much for your help.
Kindest regards,
Kyra Cox

He replies:

Dear Mrs Cox

I apologise for the delay in answering your question. It took a while, but gave me the opportunity to discuss your father's case with one of our transplant surgeons who has worked for a couple of years in Australia and therefore knows transplantation medicine here & there from the inside.

With respect to your questions, the following: in principle, it would be possible for your father to continue here. I presume that we run the same kind of tests when screening a patient for transplantation. Most likely, these would not need to be repeated. In your father's case, the status of the liver tumour needs re-evaluation from time to time (we typically repeat the CT scan of liver & lungs every 3 months), but undoubtedly this is being done in Australia as well. Apart from this, your father would be seen by an anaesthetist, a transplant surgeon, and by a hepatologist, after which a formal decision to accept your father could be made. Apart from that, he would have an interview with the transplant nurse and social worker.

Waiting lists work differently in Holland compared with (what I know of) the Australian system. In your system, each transplant centre has its own donor region. In case a donor becomes available, the transplant team determines which patient will receive the donor liver. This will be determined by the perceived urgency. We have a national list containing patients from the 3 Dutch liver transplant centres. The position of patients on the waitlist is determined by the American MELD system. This scoring system is used to measure illness severity in liver transplant candidates. It uses three laboratory values (bilirubin [the parameter for jaundice], creatinine [a measure of kidney function] and INR [a measure of blood clotting]) to calculate a score that is predictive of the risk of death within three months on the liver waiting list. At the time when he was in Holland, your father's MELD score was relatively low, but this may have changed – he might now occupy a 2nd or 4th position, depending on his numbers. This MELD system is not fair to patients like your father in whom the function of the liver does not adequately reflect their risk (one may have normal lab values yet harbour a very deadly tumour). Therefore, under certain conditions patients with liver cancer may receive an 'upgrade', that is bonus points, which puts patients higher on the list. As a drawback, this bonus is only given after a minimum of 6 months on the list.

You should know that the position on the list is not all-determining. It often happens that a liver is not accepted or not suitable for the first patient waiting on the list, or that a specific transplant centre has no capacity to do the transplant (as they are busy doing one, or have no ICU bed available, etc). On the other hand, only 7% of our population have blood group B; this is higher in Australia (because of the Asians, among whom B is much more frequent). Waiting times for a B liver might therefore be shorter over there, especially when high up the list. In Holland (as in Australia, as far as I know), we do not prioritise on the cause of liver disease. If we have good reason to expect that alcohol will not cause problems, the patient will be treated just like the others. Patients who are truly addicted to alcohol will not be accepted for transplantation.

I realise that a waiting list is a morbid kind of lottery, and nobody can tell with certainty what offers the best chances to your father. Yet, my colleague and I are convinced that there is no reason to believe that he will be transplanted earlier here than he would be in Australia. The level care in Australia is excellent (I have seen detailed results of two centers, and according to my colleague they are 'typical').

And finally, as I most likely have told your father before, this waiting time is a horrible experience, and I myself would prefer the relative comfort of my 'own' country and the presence of my close relatives and friends.

More explicitly, the only reason to advise your father to come here would be if the chances of finding a donor in Australia would be judged to be poor. In that case, I expect that the team caring for your father would contact us (or any other team they would judge appropriate); I would do the same for my patients (it happens sometimes).

At this time I wish you, and of course your father strength and courage. I hope the transplant will be soon.

Sincere regards – Aad van den Berg

I respond to this generous doctor's email:

My daughter Kyra, showed me your extraordinary detailed answer to her letter. Many, many thanks. You are a remarkable person and I feel extremely honoured and grateful for the attention you've given us. You've also made it easier for me to decide what to do and where to go. From all accounts it's better and more sensible to stay here, be patient and hope for the best. That I've come this far is already a miracle of sorts. In a few weeks they're doing some more tests, x-rays and scans. We shall keep fighting the good fight!

Warmest regards

Paul Cox

This correspondence speaks for itself. The surgeon who's been so generous with his time – with his concerns, is a rare individual.

ॐ

Some ten years ago I made a film called *Molokai – The Story of Father Damien*. Father Damien was a Belgian priest who at the end of the nineteenth century went to Hawaii as a missionary. He lived among the sufferers of leprosy, caught the disease himself and died among the people he loved. Yesterday, 11 October, he was canonised and after ten years of fighting with the producers, my version of the film was shown on various European TV stations. They often say there's justice after all, but this is more like a miracle. Nobody could tell me where this version of the film came from, as the producer went bankrupt – so miracles exist after all.

A few years ago, I wrote a small contribution for a collection of essays called 'My One True Love'. Last night before I fell into a dreamless sleep, the man in the story appeared to me – waved from the distance, smiled and then turned back towards the mountains. I'm exorcising him from my life and death by repeating the story here. I don't relate to the ending any longer. I don't love my imminent demise. I want to live.

MY ONE TRUE LOVE

For the one true love of my life I want to embrace a rather large picture.

The largest of them all. A thing called death. Please read on …

The first five years of my life during the Second World War, I witnessed nothing but death and destruction. Half the population of the small town we lived in perished.

I was always immensely relieved when I came home and our house was still standing and our neighbours still alive. It caused me and others who had crawled from under the ruins a profound fascination with death and decay.

I kept looking for the skull behind the face. A rather indulgent preoccupation. It wore me out.

But I was extremely fortunate. Found a profession in which I could express myself, learned to treasure life and always tried hard to give both the good and the bad my loving understanding.

Many years later, I met an old man in Nepal with a mission. I met him seemingly by chance – yet I wonder … He was a noble Italian gentleman with a great passion for beauty and the arts. We shared a meal in a small restaurant. An old shepherd sang songs from the mountains and children offered flowers.

It was one of those evenings that helped you change.

Before we parted he said, 'When the time comes we must be able to will ourselves to death.'

He quoted Rilke:

> I would like to walk
> Out of my heart
> Under the wide sky

Then he said 'Adieu, my friend,' and disappeared into the night.

The next morning his body was brought down from the mountain. I saw his face frozen in time and space. A marble sculpture – eyes wide open – his mouth like the Buddha – infinite and timeless – freed from all mortality.

I still see his face and I still carry the little book he gave me. It is Tagore's *Gitanjali* (Song Offerings). In it I read, 'I know I've loved this life and because of that I shall love death as well.'

I stopped looking for the skull behind the face. Tried to find the human heart. It hasn't been an easy search.

Our civilisation of instant gratification is so out of touch with death that most people one meets have never seen a dead body. Many die by themselves in a white sterile room, drugged out of their minds, surrounded by strangers. There's also always some miraculous excuse for death. Recently I heard that a ninety-seven-year-old man died of cancer. I think he died because he was very old and very tired. May he rest in peace.

We seem to have taken the wrong turn. We don't understand life any more, or love for that matter, and consequently are out of tune with death. Death as we know it now is spending our earnings on things we don't need. Death is the manufacturing of guns, bombs and land mines. Things no one needs. Death is building cities as drab and grey as possible. Death is emptying the oceans of life and polluting our rivers and waterways. Death is celebrating the wrong gods for the wrong reasons. Death is denying our children to dream of the future. Death is the politics of greed, hatred and ignorance. Death is lost to the living.

My friend from the mountains was right. Poverty and nakedness and even death are nothing, provided there is tenderness, provided we've learned to live without fear.

In the face of death everything becomes more humane, more alive. In the face of death only true love makes sense – harmony, peace, warmth, gentleness, kindness, words that have almost disappeared from our vocabulary. All the ambitions, all the career moves become meaningless. In the face of death we can find our true spirit.

All we have to do is return the key and our claims to the house and maybe expect some kind words from families and friends. No more noisy, loud words. 'People deal in whispers near the dying,' says Tagore. Now we have time for ourselves and can think of all those we have loved and how we have loved them. Life could be like that …

Oh yes, death is my true love. The true love of my life. I couldn't live without it.

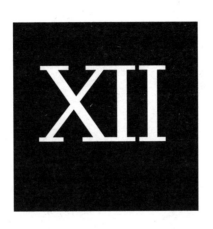

There's a long queue of people standing in a cobbled street. A murky river flows past and a rusty bridge hangs in the sky. Somebody is handing out livers. Happy-looking people are coming out of a small building, all carrying plastic bags with dripping livers. When I ask someone what he's going to do with his liver and how he's going to replace his old liver, the man screams out, 'Don't ruin it for me!' A woman says, 'I'm beautiful and transparent.' I'm told to stand in line and wait my turn, but I realise that they've almost run out of livers and it would be a waste of time to wait for one. The liver recipients are bouncing them in the street, like beach balls. 'This is how you reactivate them,' says a man in a fur coat. I walk towards a river and, together with many who've missed out, start looking for pieces of wood or bamboo to make a fishing rod. They use bits and pieces of an old, lifeless liver as meat for bait. Large fish appear – jumping in and out of the water. A feeling of hopelessness engulfs me. I don't belong here – nobody does. I wake up and have an extremely hot shower to get rid of the horrible frustration that dream left in my consciousness.

అఃఅ

Had Kyra and Marius here for a meal. Marius cooked a splendid dinner and we joked and enjoyed each other's company. Marius lives on a different planet and doesn't notice domestic duties or what it takes to keep the house and office going without an income. I overreact to one of his comments and become angry. Have totally forgotten what his comments were. He's only twenty and I shouldn't get angry with him. Such a rare occasion that we can sit together, but I ruined everything without giving it a second thought. This is how my own father destroyed my childhood. Yes, after five months on the waiting list, playing that horrible waiting game, my emotions are not fully under control – but to take it out on my son whom I adore and love is extremely disturbing. I'm full of remorse and if he hadn't left the house I would ask him to understand and forgive me right now. I've always been the so-called breadwinner, the man in charge, always took the initiative and made sure I lived up to expectations, but now I can't stand the responsibility any more – I don't want to look ahead because I still see nothing there and I don't want to look after people any more. But all this is no excuse for such lack of faith and lack of self-control. Of course, later we embrace, forgive and forget. This must always happen at short notice. The longer pride or anger linger, the more difficult it is to heal the wounds.

❧

A few days later, Marius and I attend a meeting of the 'pre-transplant support group'. A sound technician and his wife show us a small film she made while he was waiting for a transplant. It took them almost two years to get the transplant, while his energy levels slowly dropped. She watched him becoming sicker all the time and losing his ability and will to drive, work or socialise. His personality had changed dramatically. She thought she'd lost him, and had to cope with all the emotions around her and within her.

After the transplant, her husband recovered remarkably well. He changed back to the husband she knew, and they were extremely grateful to the hospital staff. The most striking part of her story was that when she gave her husband his mobile phone back, he started to ring everybody he knew and also the people he hardly knew. Told them how much he loved them! I wasn't surprised to hear this. Facing one's mortality seems to bring out the best in us.

More blood tests in the afternoon, and a talk with the doctor, who tells me that the latest MRI scan showed that the cancer was under control and that he didn't need to see me for three months. So I will live for at least another three months and could even receive a transplant in that time. How things have changed again. I'm trying to cope emotionally and digest this twist of fate. My greatest fear is that I will slide down on the 'Richter scale of transplants' and will have to wait even longer. I write to one of the doctors, who assures me that this isn't the case.

చురుఁ

Days come and go. It always seems to be evening. Time for an evening meal, time for an early night in bed. It never works that way. There's always some phone call or someone visiting who needs to talk or thinks that I need to talk. I thought this time would allow me to investigate my life a little more. The eternal questions still haven't been answered. It's probably quite true that we're all more interested in finding our food, shelter and human contact, than thinking too much about the purpose of life. That strange contradiction within our society. We've created a surface normality that has nothing to do with what goes on in people's lives and in their hearts. Eighty per cent of all stories on television deal with illegal activities – like theft, rape and murder. Why this fascination with all things that break the laws of Man? Only in growing older do we realise how rare and beautiful 'reality' is. We see how miraculous it is that flowers bloom in the midst of ruins. How poetry survives in the midst of oppression. What a challenge it is and how beautiful life becomes when we acknowledge the inner world of a person and balance the inner with the outer. The interior is usually more interesting and rewarding. I have no desire to escape my present reality. That's all I have left and all I must fight for.

A week before the new tests, Suzi, my old, re-discovered friend from the distant past accompanies me to the country. It is a quiet, peaceful weekend. We plant trees and listen to the rain on the roof. I arrive with a bit of a fever and pain in my legs. The fever and the pain don't go away; they slowly get worse. Back home in Melbourne, it gets so bad that I ring the hospital. The nurse hears that I'm in pain. 'Why didn't you ring straight away? Come immediately!' So, I'm now on the way to the hospital with my legs up on the dashboard nursing a deep pain and a terrible headache. I'm sitting in an almost empty waiting room with my friend Joanie, and Marius. I've known Joanie and her family for many years. We've worked together and spend much time searching flea markets and opportunity shops. I'm enormously thankful that she went out of her way to get me here. I want to thank her but she tells me to keep quiet. She has given me some pain killers and now I see the clock on the wall running approximately three times faster than normal clocks, and the people who walk in and out all move in slow motion and carry black baskets, brooms made out of twigs and speak a language that sounds medieval but hasn't got one recognisable vowel. Have we moved to a different century? Then the door opens and we're swallowed up by this huge modern hospital. A little cubicle in Emergency offers me a bed, two chairs for visitors and the hospital gown that has to be opened and closed at the back.

Doctors and nurses come and go. An extremely thorough and serious Chinese doctor seems to be in charge. The liver unit is informed, and they advise to take patient Cox upstairs and submit him to the liver department again. Kyra and her friend Peachie join us, while Joanie and Marius depart. We travel to the eighth floor. Meanwhile, the pain in my legs becomes excruciating. I try to be brave, but now and then I lose control. A homecoming of sorts when we arrive at the liver unit. In moments of despair, we must be with people we know or who know us and help when facing the void.

Kyra and Peachie finally leave me and I fall into an exhausted sleep. I wake up and see the vast city through the window. A large expanse of houses and trees – a huge park in the middle and grey-blue mountains in the far distance. This is living the high life.

Surgeons, doctors and all sorts of experts are visiting and I perceive their questions with one ear – I listen to the great multicultural diversion of the ward with the other. Three or four generations of a Vietnamese family are sitting around the bed of an elderly gentleman. Vietnamese is an extraordinary language – not as melodious and beautiful as the Italian spoken next to me, but there's a hidden richness that cannot really be appreciated by a Western person. The light across the city is slowly fading. The pain that had settled in my left leg has suddenly moved to my right leg. I can't stand on it, and visits to the toilet are almost too much. I don't want to talk any more about the things that happen to me. Boring and indulgent – unless I do something positive with the agony, the ecstasy and the pain.

Half the world is asleep. A woman with little hair has been

watching her TV set non-stop all day. It's still playing now. She may have gone to sleep behind the thin curtain and hopefully a nurse will silence the nonsense that has been spreading from this horrible little menace all day. Canned laughter, shallow voices, forced happiness! This dumb, endless flood of nothingness has the power to numb troubled souls and maybe has a purpose that way, yet it would be so easy to give programs a bit more substance, a bit more heart.

My legs are still on fire. Have tried to walk up and down the ward, but the pain got too much. The city hides in the low clouds that have come down during the night. The elderly Vietnamese gentleman has moved a chair close to the window and traces the raindrops that have attached themselves to the outside. He leans on a cushion he's taken from his bed and traces raindrops like a child. I see him focusing on the window and then staring into the distance. Maybe he thinks about his homeland, about his past, his youth in Vietnam, the violation and destruction, the endless bombs that rained from the sky. He's riddled with cancer. Not much can be done for him, I hear. I like this man very much. Wish I could tell him about my thoughts, about my love for him that is too timid to speak

ॐ

Dreamed of the mountains in Nepal. They appeared and disappeared, as I floated on crystal clear water. Some years ago I climbed one of these mountains, together with a Thai monk. When we had arrived at a small temple tucked away in the rocks, he disappeared and left me with other monks. I was forced to wait and put my life on hold. I became a prisoner of circumstance. As the landscape in front of me expanded, I grew smaller, more and more insignificant. Started to meditate on images I remembered and somehow the paintings of Johannes Vermeer, the great Dutch painter became my mandalas. They offered infinity! They had windows through which one could find infinity. Now I stare at the mountains across the city, through the hospital window, and long for the land of pictures. Vermeer is pulsating within me. How beautiful the memory of his stillness.

❦❧

Kyra and Arabella pay me a visit. Arabella is rather puzzled. What is Opapa doing in bed in the middle of the day? I want to lift her up, want to hug her, kiss her, but lifting is not possible and hugging could cause another infection. Besides, Arabella is not sure about her grandfather at all. She watches him carefully and stays well within a safe distance, close to her mother.

❦❧

The elderly Vietnamese gentleman has been told to go home. The whole family comes to pick him up. He wishes me 'good luck again'. The first time he speaks to me. It's much better than a simple 'good luck'. A woman immediately takes his bed, straight from a heavy operation. Only a week ago, I wrote how things had changed again and I thought I had three untroubled months ahead of me … Suddenly, thunder and lightning and a downpour of heavy rain. The lightning flashes past the window and erupts into thunder before it moves out of frame. The woman across is now awake and talking to a nurse about what happened to her. I shouldn't listen in, but have always been blessed with fine hearing and find it hard not to follow the various conversations around me. Manage to separate them and sometimes write down a few good lines that stick to the soul. The woman thought she had had gall bladder problems and when they checked, it was discovered that apart from a few insignificant gallstones, she had three large cancerous growths in her abdomen. They were removed immediately. The doctor told her that the gall bladder had most probably saved her life. A hospital ward teaches us how vulnerable, how terribly vulnerable we are.

怘怙

Clouds have gathered outside. A pale evening sun is struggling to get through. The woman across is asking the nurse to disconnect her oxygen mask and intravenous drip, her lifelines. Her ten-year-old daughter is coming to visit. She doesn't want her daughter to see her as a seriously ill patient in a hospital bed. The nurse says it's against the rules but she disconnects the lifelines, helps with a bit of lipstick and make-up and combs her hair. A beautiful young girl enters the ward. Weeps helplessly in her mother's arms. 'It's all right, sweetheart.' 'I'm getting better.' 'I'll be home soon, my darling.' She tenderly caresses her distraught girl. A strong shaft of light burns through the grey clouds, uniting mother and daughter. 'You must go now, darling, Daddy is waiting.' The nurse rushes in to reconnect her lifelines. Now the mother weeps, the same helpless tears.

I dream that my hospital bed is growing smaller all the time. I finish up in a foetal position, using my arms and legs to keep the sides from moving any closer. Then, as I jump out of the now extremely small space, a group of people chase me through the corridors of the house of my youth. Every time I manage to close one door, fists and boots make holes in the doors and break them down. Finally, there is no more space to hide from the world. I'm being pushed into a precipice. The only thing that prevents me from falling into the deep is the long hair of a dark woman. Fortunately, I wake up hanging out of my bed – hanging onto sheets and infusion cables for my dear little life.

In the middle of the night I write a letter to my brother.

Wim, I suddenly see you in silhouette behind the glass in the corridor. Please come in, my dear friend. There're four sick people here but you know me – you know me very well. I'm the one who sits straight up in bed attached to some tube that dances as I write. You will soon enter – will hang your coat in the hall and in your low voice I hear you say, 'I am his brother, can I go in?' And I say to the nurse, 'He's the brother of my life. My only brother. A special man. All shades of light pass through his eyes. He's a poet and a lover of life. My brother!' Then you sit next to me here in the dark in this large hospital on the other side of the world. 'I've missed you. How are you? How was the journey? I love you.'

No, no tears – even though they silently flow like rivers

– there's nothing we can do with them. We can't do anything either with all the flowers that are spread across the room. People receive flowers before they die. You can never tell anyone about your pain. You understand, dear Wim, and take the pain away from me. We shared much agony when we were children. I am not going to die dear Wim. The whole night we sit together, holding hands. Morning light filters through the room. The mountains in the distance are catching the first light. 'Time for us to part'. See you very soon. Keep faith – give my love to all those who love me. I try to walk with you to the door, but don't make it. Please don't worry, dear Wim. I'm not alone any longer and want to see you again in this life. Please tell our mother – how long has she been gone from us – that I've always loved her terribly much. She gave us our humanity and our vulnerability. She understood creative freedom and respect for all creatures – dead or alive – big or small. Wish I could dream of one more film. It would be set in space. I love you, Wim.

Paulus.

ੵੵ

'Art rather than ethics constitutes the essential metaphysical activity of Man,' says Friedrich Nietzsche. I don't know why I remember this now. This is my fifth day in hospital. The pain has subsided a fair bit, and I'm just waiting for the doctors to examine me. I need to get back on the transplant list as soon as possible.

A male nurse with a strange accent has pulled a curtain right around my bed. I don't think he understands the word 'view' because every time I tell him not to close the curtain completely and leave the view exposed, he closes the curtain even more. I've heard him having conversations with various people in the ward. He's eager and helpful, but doesn't listen to anyone. All advice is ignored. He's eager and helpful and very funny because he doesn't listen to anyone. I'm trying my utmost to ignore him. It hurts too much when I laugh.

The TV set in the corner starts to spit out its horror and nonsense. Fortunately, the sound is right down, but my hearing is too alert. Several times I hear someone say, 'The American people'. Don't know what program it is, but when I hear 'the American people', 'the Australian people' and so on, I know that nationalist ideas have no future. They must retreat. Individualism should fill the vacuum. If humankind wants to have a future we have to stop marching behind flags. Pride and love for one's country and heritage is a different thing all together. When Man walked on the Moon, he left the American flag behind. That was a big mistake. It should've been the flag of humankind – the flag of all nations … And the conversation with the man who cheated and lied and threw more bombs on Vietnam than all the bombs that were dropped in the Second World War – Richard Nixon – should never have occurred. The astronaut should have spoken to a child somewhere and said, 'I'm in the universe and I love you.'

I'm reading three books at the same time. In between, I try to write these tales, although they get increasingly more difficult to complete. What goes on inside? Will I be alive in a few months' time – will I be alive next week? Will I be the recipient of a new liver before Christmas? Or will I die before any of this happens? I knew that something was in store for me, but never thought my legs would blow up and refuse to carry my body.

❧

I have been here now almost six days. Persistent rumours tell me that I will be able to go home tomorrow. What a lovely thought. I will hopefully be back on the transplant list and start the waiting game again. Somebody with my blood group will have to die and be a willing donor. It's hard to imagine if that will ever happen. If it doesn't, I will have to depart from this life at some stage. I was prepared and ready before, but not any more. As I depart from the three women I have shared the ward with, there's a sudden warmth and intense human contact. People on the edge are so much more human. These women are courageous and caring. They don't complain, and smile and weep without holding back.

Today, a full-body bone scan. 'Avoid contact with children and pregnant women.' This is the second time for me. I'm sitting in the Nuclear Department, waiting my turn.

Two large women are fighting in the waiting room. Mother and daughter.

Daughter: 'I'm getting out of here.'
Mother: 'Don't be so stupid.'
Daughter: 'You're being stupid.'
Mother: 'Don't call me stupid, I am your mother.'
Daughter: 'You called *me* stupid.'
Mother: 'No, I didn't.'
Daughter: 'Yes, you did.'

A nurse enters, calls the daughter's name and both disappear into the corridor.

What am I doing here? Why am I here? Please, Lord Buddha, take me away from these people in white coats and loud footsteps in endless empty corridors. Now I find myself in a scanning device that slowly travels across my body and soul. I keep my eyes closed and think of the Cévennes Mountains near my home in France, or what I perceive to be my home.

Christmas 2009. My grandchild of almost three wants to know more about the chiming of a clock and how it could speed up the arrival of Christmas. We wait for an old 'repeater' to strike seven times, and count them. I then explain to her that this clock is called a repeater and would strike again in two minutes' time. She suddenly disappears, and I think this isn't really interesting to her. But she returns with a container and places it in front of the clock.

'What are you doing, Arabella?'

'I'm catching Time, Opapa!' And indeed the seven new strikes are carefully caught in flight and stored in the container. She then generously offers me some time in the future when needed.

Around this time last year, I was in South Australia visiting James Currie and his family. Jim is one of my oldest friends, and has been the sound designer on most of my films. We trust and love one another like brothers and have been on the movie trail in many different countries. When New Year's Eve arrived, we drank a toast, looked out over the dark ocean and made plans for the New Year.

The celebration certainly didn't live up to expectations. A month later, I was told I had limited time and wouldn't see Easter. But I'm still here, watching the Christmas celebrations with amusement. I always feel even more of an outsider during Christmas. Partly because of childhood memories, partly because of a certain absurd character called Father Christmas. An elderly man with a cottonwool beard who brings goodwill and presents to bewildered children and then promotes rampant consumerism, which instead of peace and goodwill, celebrates ignorance and greed. I don't put this very well, but my fellow non-believers will certainly understand what I am trying to say.

On the nightly news it is reported that the people this year have spent $3 billion on Christmas goodies. 'A disappointing result compared with last year,' says the newsman. Please, Father Christmas, could I have three snowflakes, five raindrops and … if possible one large passing cloud. Thank you so much. In Vietnam they made a small treaty – no killings, please, during Christmas Day.

✂✐

Angeline and Jaap are flying to Australia from Holland. Due to bad weather they're delayed and I'm given a bit more time to put the house in order. Wish I could order my thoughts and my emotions as well. I feel uncertain and trapped. There's something happening somewhere of relative importance to my life. Nearby, people are having dinner. Their voices are growing louder as more alcohol is consumed. Their laughter has little joy; it echoes through the streets and hurts my nerves. I should be pleased – and of course I am – that I'm still here – that Christmas will be shared with people of my own blood, that I exist – yet I feel alone and hurt. I'm searching for a ray of light, a loving hand, a sense of future. Christmas was always a difficult time. I get homesick without knowing where home is.

My sister and brother-in-law are still asleep after the long journey. I'm preparing a little lunch for us all and Kyra is assembling the children's stove that Father Christmas and Company left for Arabella. The little girl is thrilled and prepares us all instant meals via the utensils that came with the stove. In the afternoon we sleep some more and then get ready to have dinner at my friends Asher and Luba Bilu's place, nearby along the ocean. Suzi decides to join us. A wonderful Indian meal cooked by their friend Kabita from Kolkata is waiting for us.

My phone rings several times and various text messages from all over keep me busy during dinner. 'I'm sorry, but I have to keep my phone on in case the hospital rings.' It's a warm and wonderful evening. We laugh and joke. It doesn't occur to me at all that it's amazing to have part of my own family sharing this meal. I'd never thought this could happen. Is this our last supper?

I tell Suzi that I feel a bit strange. As if an invisible curtain surrounds me and follows me wherever I go. When I stretch my arms I can almost touch the curtain, which has become a wall of stone still invisible and further away from me.

Asher proclaims that a woman in Rome has 'gone down' on the Pope. Apparently there was a newsflash where a woman jumped a barricade and brought His Holiness down before any of the security people could stop her. I say, 'We all have metaphysical needs,' and the phone rings. It's now 11.35pm, time to go home. 'Is that Paul?' 'Yes.' 'Good evening.' It's a female voice and I wonder who is ringing at this hour. 'Hope you had a good Christmas. This is Julie from the Austin

Hospital. Can you come to Emergency as soon as possible? We think we have the right liver for a transplant.' My first thoughts are, 'This can't be happening now, they've made a mistake, for heavens sake!' Then meekly I hear myself say, 'Yes, I'll be there. Thank you.' After seven months of waiting and living with the mobile phone as a lifeline, and time slowly eating away hope and future, something enormous is about to happen. For a while we all sit in bewilderment. Angeline, Jaap and Suzi drive me to the hospital. We stop at my apartment first and I fill a bag with essentials. Later it is discovered that none of the items gathered are useful or made any sense.

I'm writing this now in the hospital. I've already gone through the routine of X-rays and tests. Now I can only hope with all my heart – with all my might – that all this is going to succeed. After the initial shock, I'm at peace. This is the only chance I have. Don't know for how long I could have continued. My instinct had told me already – not long, dear friend. You're rolling down the hill, closing up; the end of the show is nigh. Surrender with grace and dignity.

An anaesthetist from South Africa appears. He tells me what is going to happen. There is no more doubt now: I'm in for a liver transplant. I sign a form and then a tall doctor called Saskia guides me into the operating theatre. 'Saskia was Rembrandt's wife,' I say. 'Yes, that's right. That's how I got my name – I'm Dutch.' I touch her hand, 'May Rembrandt be with us.'

I wake up – from where? From what? Feel nothing. See nothing. A flock of birds flees my body. Someone enters my cage, two nuns walk past. 'Large white wings of desire,' says a man on a duck-shaped bicycle. The bicycle or duck bites a passing horse. Other animals laugh at the horse that has been bitten. More horses gallop past, all laughing – showing big white teeth. Within each tooth is a waterfall, brilliantly lit from inside. 'They are only joking,' says a Russian sailor, and I wonder how I can understand Russian. 'When you listen, everything can be understood,' says a nurse. The earth trembles, shifts and moves. I know that deep underground worms are building a road from within the earth. How clever can you get? It's time to open the wooden door to the opera house. 'How do you feel?' Good! Good as gold. And yes – the more you buy, the more you save. But wait, there's more. Volcanoes spewing oil into the air. The oil catches fire and lashes like a whip across the horizon. Then comes down like a complete burning galaxy. What power am I part of? Someone says, 'Ants are building bridges of uncertainty.' Camels take over, control the roads. They all have gearsticks. The camels aren't happy and bite people at random. A man erects a big sign: 'Rubber plants for sale'. The sign flies away like a kite, and for a moment a serene valley opens up. Small rivers and bridges, medieval sceneries with sun-drenched gardens and children on ice skates. There's a feeling of togetherness upon the cobblestones. What can you do with death? Someone holds my hand. 'Where are you?' 'In Venice, the year is 1473.' 'You might be there, but I'm not,' says a voice. 'How can I be in Venice and you're not?' 'That's the problem we're trying to solve here.' The true facts of life are felt and understood by very few,' I say. Dark beasts: lions, panthers, tigers – some can fly, others leave trails of fire behind. They don't attack me – maybe try to scare me. 'We all have a function in life. To find out what this is can take a lifetime. Some people have a 'calling' and excuse bad behaviour as part of their calling. 'I've been called to kill you – just doing my duty.' 'Thank you, sir, much appreciated.'

Now floating in that large empty space between gruesome pain and madness. I notice that there are tubes everywhere and pumps that beep. My arms are blue. The Bolivian Army has sent a film team to use the same sets as we've used in a different film. A captain on an iron structure shaped like a horse says that these films do all right once they've killed all the stars. I don't know whether he's part of the army or the film people. There's a picture of me when I am 143 years old. I know they cheated to try to keep me alive. Chris Haywood and Aden Young are sitting on a donkey, announcing the arrival of the final days of shooting. Where's the group photo and the make-up department? The real dream is now. People are happy for me. Why? I'm disturbed – in pain – feel a terrible sense of loss.

Music, voices, endless conversations. I can't face it. All has gone dark. 'Try to stay away from the dreams,' says a man in a long black coat. He must be a Venetian doctor. We walk along the cobblestones along the murky river of my youth and enter a market with all types of chandeliers made out of teeth. One can buy sets of false teeth with brilliant single waterfalls in every tooth. 'Vivaldi used to live here,' says the doctor. 'He will live here,' I say because the year is 1473 and this is a few centuries too early. Vivaldi lived in Venice from 1678 to 1741. I know and remember the dates, because we almost made a film on Vivaldi's life. A rather solid type of logic has control now, except there's a hole in the ground with a huge worm trying to get out. The doctor has turned into a monkey. For a while I think it was just a costume change. Children are flying balloons. What reality is this? There are no balloons in 1473. I want to ask them, how and where they got these balloons, but as I approach, I notice these balloons are animal bladders, held up high in the sky by long sticks. More balloons appear above the houses along the canals – they must be held up by extremely long sticks. No, that's not possible. These must be real balloons, but they can't be real balloons! The confusion makes me sick. I realise I'm lying in a bed, in a hospital. 'Help me, please help me! Please hold me, I am dying.' Where's the nurse whose presence makes me feel sane and at home? Please come and help me. Kyra walks past. I recognise her voice. She speaks different languages. From the tone of her voice she ages and grows younger again. The sky is full of arrows. A few of them penetrate my body. The pain is horrendous. It's easy to let go now. To slip via that large empty space into total lunacy. *Allegro Non Troppo*. Who's the man that made this film? I know him; met him years ago – Bruno Bozzetto. I want to tell him, I now understand your film.

There's much relief – euphoria. People are happy I'm alive. I'm improving. I feel grieved to the core – that great grief of Man. All has closed in. It took a lot to get on the liver transplant list. What a relief it was for me and my children to be told one day that I was on the list. You're given a bit of hope – a little light appears. Then the waiting game, in which one slowly starts to realise that your chances are actually very low – that an infection can strike at any time or other problems develop. People die or get sicker waiting for a transplant because the donor situation is so very, very poor, especially in Australia. Some religious leaders teach and believe that it's against God's wishes to leave your organs behind, to save other people's lives. It doesn't make sense – it doesn't add up. On the day of judgement we're all going for a stroll to the village square – it doesn't look good if liver, heart or kidneys are missing. God tolerates abuse of various organs but no donations, please. Missing organs would make a mockery of the Act of Creation! Allegro Non Troppo …

After three days in Intensive Care, I am taken to my ward. Someone has just died, either in this bed or next door. A woman is sobbing quietly. She weeps right through the nightmare that follows. I sit for hours staring at a blank page. What is left to record? What is left to say?

Some footage has been taken during the last three hours of the operation. The surgeons talk to camera with my blood on their masks. What heroes these people are. 'The liver of a young person, who died suddenly – the perfect fit for Paul.' I am lying like a cadaver: arms outstretched, colourless flesh, one big open wound. How is all this possible? They continue, 'The longer that Paul was on the waiting list, the greater the chance that he might have a catastrophe while waiting, and might never make it. His own liver was full of tumour, hard like a brick and very scarred. We believe that the cancer was entirely within the liver, and we are very optimistic that Paul has been cured by the operation. He won't have cancer any more, and of course he won't have hemochromatosis, because the new liver will be processing all the iron. It's a wonderful gift for Paul, from another family that is going through a terrible time. The family agreed that the patient could be a donor. He contributed his liver, kidneys, pancreas, his heart and lungs. Seven people benefited from this extraordinary gift. It is for Paul, and the other recipients, a gift of life.'

On my hallucinatory journey through the centuries, one of the nurses accompanied me to Venice. She had a stillness and grace that was not of this time. I saw her crossing a bridge, talking to a woman who was selling vegetables near the water, and then opening a solid wooden door with a large key to let us both in. All this happened in 1473. In reality, she had guided me silently through the drafty corridors of the Nuclear Department and stood by when a large scanning device investigated the new liver. I was cold and in pain, felt distressed and was immensely thankful that she was nearby. I wish I could've talked to her at length. She had a presence that seemed so right and comforting; there was something old fashioned about her that made it easy to move through the dimensions of time and space.

From my window high up in the sky, I can see the city and imagine driving through the streets and becoming part of the activity again. It's overcast. A rich grey blanket lies upon the city. Birds jump off the building next door like kamikaze divers, and instead of growing smaller on the horizon they disappear instantly.

As I write this, all major tubes and attachments have been removed. A few times during the feverish nights, I try to fight the hallucinations by ripping the tubes and connections out of my body. Blood everywhere, broken bits and pieces. The poor nurses heroically rebuild the structures that keep me breathing, screaming, dreaming, bleeding, feeding, crying, laughing and remembering.

You look good. How do you feel? Merry Christmas to you too. People have been so supportive. They mean so well, but each confrontation with a visitor confirms the fact that we have no ability at all to communicate our feelings through words. Indeed. 'What can you say to him when you know what he's gone through?' Best is to look at people's eyes, hold their hands, touch their faces. All through my cancer year, I've been trying to wind down the clock – find the core of my existence. Floated in and out of this world and the journey of my star. Returned to the early years of my youth. All the killing and destruction that went on during the war while I was becoming a human being with a mind and a heart and a conscience. Then the grim years after the war. There was only one street in my small border town in Holland that wasn't broken up or riddled with potholes. Polished floors or streets that reflect the sky still make me feel uncertain.

I was shy with a longing for beauty and justice. Escaping to Australia gave me a sense of purpose and a way of coping with the memories of the madness and the sadness of my youth. My brother Wim went to Germany – I had to go to the other side of the world to attempt to escape our past. Australia helped me to free myself from those haunting shadows, and my confidence increased. Australia helped me believe in my spirit and not be afraid of those darker forces that linger inside. Then the years as a filmmaker and the constant travelling around the world. Success was about the worst thing that could happen. But it did happen and it threw me into great turmoil. Then both Norman Kaye and I suffered severe breakdowns after the international success of *Man of Flowers*. We just couldn't cope. But I must admit that I did appreciate the first stirrings of some appreciation. It helped me to simply grow up.

Norman died five years ago. He was not only an amazing friend but somehow we grew up together. When we first met he was forty five and I was thirty two. I admired him as a musician and not as an actor. 'Stop acting' was one of our standard jokes. He did stop acting and became 'real' very real indeed. We gave one another trust and love and understanding and consequently we both soared. Norman appeared in most of my films. Even if there was no part for him I would find some reason to have him around. I still miss him, especially now as the crows gather for an evening discussion in a tree below my window. The cypress and beech trees that lead to the cemetery on the hill are still glowing in the rapidly fading light. Another night closes in. Darkness will be hidden in darkness. A single body of a single woman emerges from a clutter of graves. She's wrapped in a blanket of straw. A flash of lightning – a clap of thunder. The gods retreat. Night has come.

Rabindranath Tagore wrote, 'I know I've loved this life and because of that I shall love death as well.' When I first travelled to the East, I landed in the dark at Calcutta airport. It was in the times of the Naxalites – young communists who tried to change the system and were brutally suppressed. There were no streetlights along the way from the airport, only small fires that gave some idea of what was beyond. In front of my $5-a-night hotel were many bodies, sleeping on the footpath. The next day, together with Sheila, an American student I'd met on the bus, I went to a lecture on Tagore at Calcutta University. In the morning I'd seen a van collecting dead bodies from outside my hotel and was a little reluctant to go to Tagore's celebration. A sadhu in the street had already told me that life was an illusion. All fate, no choice. So it must have been fate that lead me to Tagore. Anil Acharya, a young student, emerged from the crowd and started to talk to us. Anil is still my friend, part of my family. I think of him and his wife, Sahana, and all the adventures we shared later. India always gave me hope and peace. My real 'growing up' happened there. Despite the raging poverty and often terrible injustice, India is a giving place. Now I would love to sit on the banks of the Ganges and watch the world drifting by. The very thought makes me feel better, makes me want to escape this concrete womb.

৵৶

It's twelve days now since the transplant. A woman has been screaming all night in great agony. A strange howl that only stops out of sheer exhaustion in the morning. I hear she's one hundred years old and doesn't understand English. Where does she come from? What sort of youth did she have? What memories does she carry? I'm on the other side of the corridor, but her cries have penetrated and linger. She's so alone it hurts. Now I can hear the rattling of the tea wagon and all the early morning confusion. Do I still know my body? The new liver doesn't have my DNA. But I think this is more – a metaphysical matter. Yesterday I was asked what my thoughts were when I woke up from my journey into the void. I tried to explain that I had no thoughts – that this question is silly and should never be asked.

A woman sits on my chest. She knows it hurts, then moves down and starts to make love to me. This hurts too, but she doesn't care. She says I'm lucky, because she has developed a system where she can cut organs out of people's bodies while keeping them alive. 'Think of the benefits. You of all people should appreciate this. We will cut your head into four pieces, while you're fully conscious. It's a world first.' She produces a small saw and starts to draw lines on my face and skull. 'You're going to kill me!' 'I thought you would live up to your promise to be a good donor. Now stop talking and lie still. Firstly we're going to cut your face in half.' There's a screwdriver on the floor close to my right hand, if I could only get hold of it. She's now sitting on my wound and the saw is in place. The pain is excruciating. Some magic force puts the screwdriver in my right hand and with all my might I stab her through the left temple. The screwdriver goes right through her head; two eyes pop out and hit the floor. They're being picked up by a small electric van with a sign: 'Spare parts and other delicacies.' The woman through her distorted bleeding face says, 'Bravo, now you're getting strong enough to let us harvest your organs without fuss.' She looks terrible. She bites off her tongue and hurls it, along with the eyeballs, into the van. This is a horrible dream – I never dream like that, but some of the drugs are mean spirited and drag you along.

ও×ৎ

Today the first few setbacks. There is indeed talk of going home, but there are new tests to be done and I need to stay a few more days and nights in my cage with a view. I am immensely thankful that my sister Angeline and Jaap are here. They came to share Christmas and say goodbye. Instead they became part of the transplant miracle. They visit me every day and keep an eye on my home. We are all so bewildered that we make silly jokes that make me hysterical. I have to beg Jaap to stay away from my room. Laughing is impossible. His dry humour is a real threat to my new liver.

New dreams invade my universe. Maudie Palmer and I are carrying metal constructions into a building that has much bad art on display. People are raving about the exhibition. I can't remember the art, only some of the fancy titles. *Three Pieces of Toilet Paper on a String, Violin Without Moustache, Tea Time in Paradise, The Monk Who Couldn't Say No or Yes.* There were many more, but they have disappeared into the mist. The piece Maudie and I brought in is also on display. Part of it is a backlit surface with a face appearing through a highway. The face looks familiar. Maudie whispers, 'This is my self-portrait.' Then a big woman with a ring through her nose – like a New Guinea highlander – says that she's sold the Maudie portrait, and no discussion can take place until she has received her commission.

The day outside looks clear. I hear it's over forty degrees. There are cars moving in and out of small tunnels. People are visiting the dead. A small helicopter hovers above. The crows are busy in the sky, and appear much closer to my window than before. No sound from the outside penetrates. The soundtrack comes from the corridors of the hospital. A strange mixture of metallic despair and routine desperation.

⊷⊶

I've been home for a few days. Today it's twenty days since the transplant. The pain hasn't improved, but at least I can move about and slowly claim bits and pieces of my life again. A horrendous back pain overshadows the pain in my chest. Strong painkillers have been recommended and help a bit. But I will return to Venice if I'm not careful and maintain distance from the morphine.

It has taken a week or so to find the concentration to write a few things down again. Today I manage to walk to the park nearby – cross the road, which is a bit scary, and sit on an old park bench watching the grass and the trees and the people with their children strolling past. It is lovely to smell the air, to feel that things are alive around me – that I am part of all this. I ring my dear friend Tessa who lives nearby and I try to explain on her answering machine my joy about being free and, for a change, on my own and enjoying the park. I didn't get very far, as the simple description of the large tree in front of me moves me so much that I choke with gratitude and, when I recover, the answering machine has run out. How rich simple pleasures can be. When the light starts to change, I slowly return home, and feel enriched and beautifully alive.

ॐ∞

My brother Wim is the next person to look after me for a few weeks. He's arrived from Germany and I'm immensely relieved that he's here. He represents my family, my past. We hardly knew one another as we grew up. Every moment of the day or night that I feel well enough, we talk. We connect. We bleed willingly without making a face. We never had much time together. It's remarkable to discover that both of us haven't changed very much. We're still a little shy and oversensitive. He helps me heal and I'm very grateful. I observe him gently. 'Dearest Wim, I love your goodness and grace. We've travelled a long way to find each other again.' Wim calls the new liver 'our soul brother'. We go to the hospital and visit a 'slice of my old liver'. It's wrapped in plastic, floating in liquid. A dark slice of meat with holes in it. Through a microscope we see a deserted landscape with iron ore. It looks like an Aboriginal sand painting. For a moment we hold hands as we try to find our way out of the hospital. 'Tonight we'll have a vegetarian meal,' says my brother.

Yesterday, I met a few fellow recipients in the waiting areas of the hospital. We so easily talked and understood one another. They all agreed that the transplant experience had made them more aware human beings, and had changed their appreciation of life. There was a great loving atmosphere, and I thought about all these wonderful people being dead if transplants hadn't become available in the last twenty to twenty-five years. If we all thought of ourselves, or our loved ones, as potential recipients, we could build a greater public awareness and probably live in a more compassionate world.

I have dinner with another liver recipient. She fell ill one day and two weeks later woke up with a new liver. Her story is heroic and harrowing. The pain, confusion and despair I experienced waiting for a transplant, happened to her in retrospect. Both of us had little chance to survive. Yet here we are. Our survival instincts connected. We're talking, laughing, crying, telling ghost stories and then walking through the rain hand in hand. We kiss goodbye, like other people do, and all that grief – that great grief of mankind – evaporates. We are alive, more alive than anyone around us, with our matching scars and tears of gratitude. Her parting smile stays deeply embedded in my heart.

☙❧

Since I was discharged I've been re-admitted to hospital twice. Today I come for a check-up, and am told by a warm and compassionate nurse, 'You're not getting out of here.' So once again I find myself in a hospital gown with new attachments, new uncertainties, new infections and fluctuating fevers. It's the same floor again, except the view is different. Rain has been lashing the window, and now sudden rays of intense sunlight turn the rain into gold. Many tell me that this is just a small step backwards. All will be fine. I've gone through too much now to ever consider defeat. Dreams and memories invade my fragile soul again. It's not always possible to separate them. Right through the night I heard a voice, a soft whispering voice, calling my name. In my sleep or dream I answered, 'Yes, Mama, I am here.' The voice was tender, warm and comforting. When I awake, I can still hear her voice. Don't try to answer, afraid it will stop.

Now sitting between my bed and the window. An evening sun has thrown long shadows via the blinds onto the floor and across my writing pad. The shadows look like bars from a prison cell. Whether I'm in jail or not it's so lovely to sit in the sun – to see the blue of the sky, to feel the world of light and shade.

I owe my friend Nate a letter. When finally there's enough energy and time, my mind doesn't respond, and for quite some time I've been staring at an empty piece of paper. We've been corresponding for years. There's an unspoken appreciation of each other's guilt complex. This is where Jews and Catholics excel. We are experts in personal guilt – collective guilt – guilty guilt – the guilt of living – the guilt of dying. Nate and I brilliantly avoid the subject and refuse to acknowledge our guilt – what guilt? And get on with our rewarding correspondence about the cinema, personal matters, politics and, of course, the future of the world. Nate is a film college professor, the director of the Roger Ebert Film Festival and a passionate teacher who allows his students to roam freely – to use their imagination instead of worrying about commerciality and profit margins. He has not only discovered some very fine new talents, but also produced their films.

We decided to work together on a film called *Who by Fire*, written by a brilliant young writer, Allison Firor. Interest was expressed by Elizabeth Taylor and Shirley Maclaine, and we thought this would easily lead to Hollywood backing. No such luck. 'Nobody is interested in ailing stars, especially when one performs in a wheelchair.'

The decision makers in Hollywood are so very, very stupid. They have no compassion, no imagination and only think in dollar signs. Because of that, they often get it wrong. What a miserable bunch of nitwits. Why do these people have a say in what our children see on the big or small screens? They still think we're talking about the sale and promotion of fast food and easy consumables. What a pity, that one of the most powerful gifts of our times is in the hands of greed, and thus blindness. Nate probably copes with all this better than I do, but suffers the same sense of injustice.

20 January. Kyra turns twenty-nine today. Little Arabella will be three in three weeks, and exactly one year ago – after having spent a horrendous night at the Emergency Department of another hospital, I am told, 'There're some spots on the liver, but they should be able to be burned off and all will be fine.'

Now I feel too weak to wonder what this year is going to bring. I am coping with a 'one day at a time' policy, and have no reason to complain. When I finally feel secure enough to believe that I'll be stationary at home. I want to find out what I've learned and then contemplate a new future. I have started this before, but now I feel fully qualified to make the past, future and present merge – to create one brilliant reality. To find reality in the unreality that surrounds us – to catch the last rays of light before they are forever lost in the rich and dangerous undergrowth of the Earth, where most mysteries and secrets wait for their moment in the sun. The short version of all this is: I will make another film.

Friends around the world prayed to Father Damien and are convinced that Father Damien saved me. They had such faith. The Nijinsky family got their dear friends to join them in a special prayer to Father Damien. In Belgium and Holland, family and friends also went to Father Damien, and in Hawaii there were many who never doubted that Damien would save me. My sisters lit endless candles to keep Damien on our side. I'm weary of religions, but not of faith. I knew there was much prayer going on, but didn't know that Damien was the focus, until Chaz Ebert and Kinga Gaspers alerted me. And who am I to doubt any of this?

There's a lot to be said for prayer – for creating positive energy. I believe in the unknown. I love the mysteries of the universe, am fascinated by all the things I don't know. Knowledge and wisdom are diametrically opposed, and so are feeling and thinking. 'We are,' answers the question, 'Why?' Since the very beginning, we've known the answers because we carried them within us. And when we forget our desire for answers or finding the right questions, we can enter a state of bliss and gratitude in which we can show our true potential as human beings and touch the planets. This adventure has touched my spirit more than my body. But if my body had perished, where would my spirit be? Maybe we've always been here – all of us – and shall always be here. Life is then a small conscious journey given to us to become, above all, richer in spirit.

A dream keeps haunting me, often returns in various

disguises. In essence it's always the same dream.

I'm lying between white sheets, attached to several lifelines. People around me are trying to keep me alive, to save me. I know death is nigh, but I feel at ease and smile at the thought that so many have faced this before me.

Then a vast infinite loneliness overcomes me. I lose my worldly consciousness and slip into a measureless space, an immense void that I vaguely recognise. Have I been here before? From where I am, I can see the Earth, cities, oceans, forests, rivers and mountains, landscapes of great beauty. I see all and everything without time, without attachments. I travel backwards through the centuries but also forward. How beautiful the Earth is. I see people working in the fields, observe them from the edge of the woods. What century is this? Who are these people? Characters that emerge from stone and dance around flames take me further back. My body becomes stone. Time and space have taken me, but my blood cries with waves of nostalgia. Music from afar touches the very core of my being.

The little face of my grandchild appears – memories of my lost youth, my mother's embrace, the mountains I see from my kitchen windows, the milky, soft bosom of my nurse. How immensely tender her white flesh. Why don't I know her name? Then the breath of my children warms my bones and my heart – they are calling me.

I return from the void, hear voices, footsteps, the chiming of clocks, bells, beeps. A hand touches my face, a warm human hand. It takes all my strength to return to the world of people, to regain consciousness. Beauty and bliss and human warmth rush through me like a potent drug. Then I wake, a few seconds have passed and I wonder.

For the very first time in many months, I attend a concert. A wonderful counter-tenor sings Vivaldi. The voice soars and holds one note that lasts a lifetime. It's so beautiful that I have to hide my tears and close my eyes. The concert hall becomes the world and I travel through time and space, then find myself back in Venice. Now I'm in the seventeenth century. The cobblestones are still there but Venice has changed. It looks much brighter and cleaner, with more stone than the wood I noticed when I hallucinated in hospital. Vivaldi is walking in front of me. It must be him because somebody nearby says, 'There goes the red priest.' But I'm not dreaming or hallucinating. I'm in a concert hall listening to 'one single note'. The nurse, who came with me to the Nuclear Department, appears again in the streets of Venice. She is now walking close by and smiling. Who is she? What does she represent? Where is she now? Should I go out and look for her?

I've written much about my imminent demise and the halo of death. I want to write about life, but that's not easy when you've been under siege and even now, while I can feel the first stirring of a new spring deep inside, I'm not quite sure about this life of ours. No, this life of ours is all right. It's the reality of our world that distorts the very essence, the truth we all feel. This civilisation doesn't celebrate life and doesn't acknowledge death. Death does not exist in a consumer's paradise and thus, neither does life.

What is life, then? Maybe life is the song of the Earth, played by the trees and falling leaves in a forest that has never been touched by Man.

Maybe life is one single raindrop, amongst the rain that has fallen upon the Earth incessantly for so many centuries.

Maybe life is the call of the nightingale, when the universe burns with stars that watch and guard all and everything on this Earth.

Maybe life just is …

Everything happens. Like rainfall or snowfall or ice melting under the sun. It happens.

Birth and death are separated by a leaf falling in autumn, a cloud passing by, a bird in flight, a train hurrying through the night, a smile, a tear, the pain of too much tenderness.

Every new day exhibits new facets of truth. New journeys into the known, the unknown and beyond. I've been very blessed and given a second chance. All I can say now is –

Life is beautiful.

EPILOGUE

Almost six months since my transplant I'm allowed to go to France. My body is healing well. The mind doesn't heal that easily. I am more and more convinced that our unconscious existence is the real one and our conscious world a type of illusion.

I return to my old farm in France. The weather is perfect. A soft breeze blows in from the mountains. The birds are building nests and the fragrance of wild flowers fills the air. The gate is open. A pathway has been cut through the long grass to the courtyard – the inner sanctum. The first thing I notice is that among the weeds, in between the old river stones, a single dark-red poppy has found a home. Against the evening sun the red becomes translucent. The wind rustles through the two cypress trees I planted long ago. They whisper, 'No more pain, no more sorrow. *La vie est belle.*'

Then the kitchen with the ancient door and that low light from the east flooding the room. I was here many centuries ago and before that. Now I am. I am here! Outside, I find the stone in the wall I once kissed goodbye. We meet again in this life, having travelled through many stages of evolution. From man to stone, from stone to man. Now I walk through the waving grass to the very edge of the land. Down below is a pathway so overgrown that only the local people can find it.

The sky is large – all embracing. The mountains glow with longing and light. A nightingale starts to sing. I am standing right in front of the world. I am the world. I am alive. I am.

ROGER EBERT is a US film critic and screenwriter. From the 1970s to 2008 he co-hosted the highly influential television program *At the Movies*. His *Movie Yearbook* is published annually. His battle with thyroid cancer has been well documented, and he continues to be an active proponent and reviewer of film. Using text to screen software he appeared on *The Oprah Winfrey Show* in 2010 to discuss his methods on coping with the loss of his voice.

JOHN LARKIN has won over a dozen national and international media awards. As a senior feature writer and daily columnist at *The Age* newspaper, Melbourne, he led many social justice and environment campaigns, and was the first Australian correspondent to cover the Ethiopan war in Eritrea, and the Somali famine. He has written books, feature film and documentary scripts, and worked with Paul Cox for several years. They are now writing screenplays for two new pictures.